PADDLING NORTH
by Audrey Sutherland

Paddling North

First edition   Printed in Canada on 100-percent recycled paper

Patagonia Books, an imprint of Patagonia Inc., publishes a select number of titles
on wilderness, wildlife, and outdoor sports that inspire and restore a
connection to the natural world.

Project Manager – Jennifer Sullivan, Joyce Macias
Editor – John Dutton
Designer – Nichole Christiani
Illustrator – Yoshiko Yamamoto
Production – Brett Piatt

Cover illustration: Yoshiko Yamamoto

Back cover inset: Audrey Sutherland Collection

Library of Congress Control Number 2012934421

ISBN 978-1-938340-02-4

TABLE *of* CONTENTS

FOREWORD

This is the story of a trip, taken over two summers, that started in Ketchikan and went all the way to Skagway. Since the first voyage, I've paddled 8,075 solo Alaskan miles and 22 more years in Alaska and British Columbia. But it is never enough. My boat now is a newer inflatable: longer, lower, and faster, with a rudder and a spray deck that sheds the rain and the seas. I have encountered thirty bears, four wolves, and hundreds of whales. We're still coexisting, and I keep learning. The philosophy is still the same. Go simple, go solo, go now.

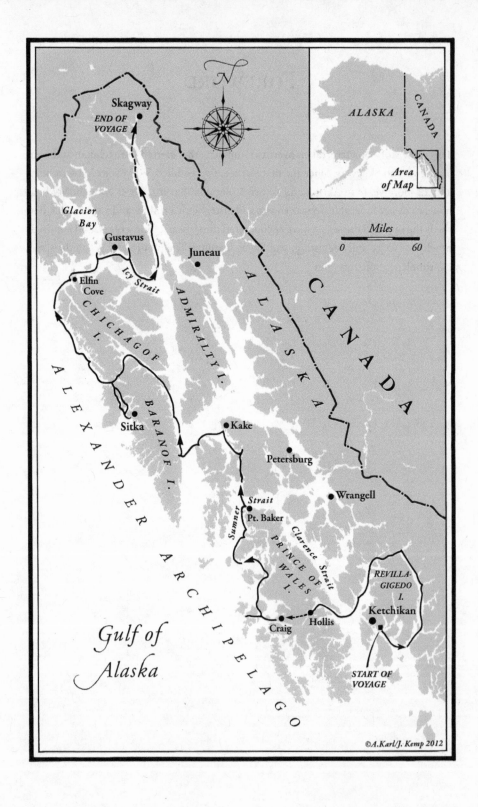

THE CHOICE

Every Alaskan has a bear story. Should I start with a true one of mine? "The grizzly bear stood there, five feet away, his enormous head visible through the thin plastic sheet over the window in the old cabin door. He was turning the doorknob with his teeth. In a moment he would burst through." Naaah, I'll tell about it later.

I first saw the 600-mile length of southeastern Alaska from the air and then on shore while on a business trip, as part of my job counseling high school students about career choices. As we landed and took off from the five main towns, I looked down on islands: tiny one-tree rocks; islets with sand beaches and coves; a 10-acre isle with a pond, huge trees, and a point for watching both sunrise and sunset; islands with no one on them.

An island is a finite thing, a concept of romance and solitude, from Calypso's island, Ogygia, in Homer's *Odyssey* to Suvarrow in Tom Neale's *An Island to Oneself*. Southeastern Alaska has more than a thousand islands. Four of the five largest towns are on islands.

For years I had searched for a combination of mountains, wilderness, and sea, and here it was. Clear quiet water, snowcapped ridges and peaks, small bays – all in the Inside Passage, sheltered from the storms of the open North Pacific. Ferries, freighters, fishing boats, and cruise ships all used it. So could I. Most of the land was within the boundaries of the 16-million-acre Tongass National Forest, the largest national forest in the United States.

There seemed be total wilderness only 10 miles away from any town, and the towns were more than 100 miles apart. That left a lot of space to paddle and explore and camp. Since 1967, between jobs, or whenever I could squeeze in a vacation, I'd been voyaging in inflatable canoes. Most of my trips had been along the more remote shores of the Hawaiian Islands: Kona, Na Pali, Hamakua, and Hana, with many along the 3,000-foot-high cliff coast that forms the north shore of Moloka'i. I'd written a book about that coast, *Paddling My Own Canoe* – now in its ninth printing. There had also been paddle trips in Samoa, Norway, Greece, Scotland, and Maine.

The choices were clear. I could paddle solo from Seattle to Skagway, an established route for fishing boats, ferries, and gold seekers. The two names together had a twangy alliteration. Both were Native American, reminders of the Haida and Tlingit people who had paddled cedar canoes for centuries along the misty shores. Skagway was a suitable destination. A classic photo showed hundreds of men toiling up the icy slopes of the Chilkoot Trail who later paddled down the Yukon River to the goldfields.

The second choice would be to go gunkholing, as boaters say, prowling in and out of tiny coves, omitting all of British Columbia for now, and instead starting at Ketchikan, the southernmost town, and meandering north to Skagway, the northernmost. I could connect a roundabout route of hot springs, old cabins, small islands, and resupply towns. I could trace parts of the historic voyages of Cook, Lisianski, Vancouver, and Muir; find the locales of some favorite books; search for mushrooms; and try to communicate with such endearing animals as whales, otters, and loons. I wasn't yet figuring to communicate with grizzly bears.

A theme to weave into the Alaska trip would be one I'd practiced on each of my previous expeditions. Part of the fun and art of long-distance paddling and camping trips has been the reverse twist of being able to carry elegant cuisine instead of gruel and granola – each week's international menu of delectable meals weighing no more than 10 pounds. In Alaska I could also add berries, mussels, and salmon.

On either route, the distance would be more than 800 miles. If I launched from Seattle, I'd be paddling north inside the protection of Canada's Vancouver Island, with cities and towns, for the first 200 miles, then following the long narrow channels to Prince Rupert. I would then recross the Canadian border and hug the shores up through the Alaska Inside Passage.

If I made the other choice, starting at Ketchikan and routing via Sitka, I'd have no cities or suburbs; there would be some inside waters, but also open sea north of Sitka. In Hawai'i, I'd had strong winds, rough seas, two-foot tides, and dumping surf, but 74-degree water, and I could hug the coast around each island. Alaska had calmer seas and rarely any breaking surf, but 48-degree water and often a range of 20 feet between low and high tide. En route to Sitka I couldn't always hug a coast. There would be four dangerous straits to cross, each one 8 to 12 miles wide. Either choice would be a race against time. I couldn't start until June, and by the end of August I needed to be back on the job in Hawai'i.

Once I'd visualized the themes and the places and put the choices into words, the decision made itself. I would go meandering, starting in Ketchikan.

My nine-foot-long inflatable canoe would be some sort of first, the smallest boat to go the distance, an impertinent toy compared to Indian cedar-log dugout canoes and modern fiberglass kayaks. It appeared to be a mocking spoofery of all serious expeditions.

"You're paddling 800 miles in Alaska in that?" said a man on the beach one day in Hawai'i.

He looked at the limp, shapeless roll of plastic on the sand. I attached the hose of the air pump to a valve. "You must be a real nut!"

The plastic canoe squirmed slowly out of its wrinkles into a tube shape. I moved the hose to the other valves.

"Where's the Donald Duck head and clown feet?"

I kept pumping. The second side and the hull assumed a boat shape, a bit like a canoe-shaped doughnut. Eighteen pounds, bright yellow, with red, white, and blue racing stripes down the sides. Its cruising speed was two knots. Racing stripes, indeed!

Why was I using this tiny boat? The answer was clear, if only to me: I already owned it; it would roll up into a duffel bag that I could take on the plane from Hawai'i; I had paddled enough rough open-ocean miles in it to know that it was sea-worthy; and, above all, it was light enough to carry by myself up the beach and above high tide each night.

My yellow color scheme was reinforced when the catalog order of foul-weather gear arrived. I put it on and walked around my Hawai'i living room. The coconut palms swayed in the warm trade winds outside, but in oilskins and sou'wester I was on deck in Conrad's *Typhoon*, battered by a cold Cape Horn sea with Dana before the mast, and racing for the America's Cup.

I laughed at the images and knew again that I had two incompatible careers. One was a full-time job: "Education Coordinator," the job description said, but I was also a vocational counselor, helping people decide what to do with their lives – which only led to my wondering whether I knew what to do with my own. The other job was roaming off to some place I'd read about, some nook of the world as isolated as I could get to, given the bounds of little money, an aversion to sponsors, and a strong preference for going alone. Recently, I'd taught a series of how-to-kayak classes for the University of Hawai'i and had given slide shows about the vagabond career.

I asked for two months' time off from the job, leave without pay. I didn't need to get "away." I needed to get "to." To simplicity. I wanted to be lean and hard and sun-browned and kind. Instead I felt fat and soft and white and mean. Years of a desk job in a bureaucracy can do that even if you like the job. Summer was a school vacation for the high school and college students and teachers I worked with, and a less busy time on my job, so the request seemed reasonable.

I ordered 24 ocean charts from the National Oceanic and Atmospheric Administration (NOAA) and 49 U.S. Geological Survey topographic maps. The topographic map for the Port Alexander C-3 quadrangle was a joy. Some musicians can look at a sheet of music and hear the melody and the rhythm. Their faces light up as they read down the page, hearing it so clearly. This map told me of the mountains and bays of southern Baranof Island.

"Look there at the head of Gut Bay," I said to myself. "You could follow the stream up to the lake, but I wonder how much underbrush there is. Look, you could bush-whack this pass over to the next lake and the next."

My excitement was building.

"That stream would take you down to the Great Arm of Whale Bay and you'd be across Baranof Island." (I found out later that small planes take this route across Baranof Island when its higher peaks and passes are clouded in.) "Plotnikof, Rezanof, and Davidof Lakes. Who were those Russians and who named the lakes? Three Forest Service recreation cabins are on the lakes, so the fishing must be good, but I can't

paddle to them or even hike. No trails and a thick forest. I'd have to charter a seaplane. Look at all the glaciers. How steep Mt. Ada is, and it's 4,000 feet high. Maybe you could climb it from this shoulder twisting up to the south from the shore of Gut Bay."

A notation on the map showed a hot spring in Gut Bay. As closely as I could from the brief description, I marked its location, along with eight others that I could reach on my meandering sea route.

My request for the two-month leave came back disapproved. I went home and looked at the Five Year Plan on the wall: income and outgo for each year, the list of important home factors, the morale-building list, the 25 things I most wanted to do in order of importance. Paddle Alaska, number one. I walked into the bathroom and looked at the familiar person in the mirror.

"Getting older, aren't you, lady? Better do the physical things now. You can work at a desk later."

The next day, I handed in my resignation, effective in two months. Sometimes you have to go ahead and do the most important things, the things you believe in, and not wait until years later, when you say, "I wish I had gone, done, kissed ... " What we most regret are not the errors we made, but the things we didn't do.

My voyage was now more open-ended, limited not by the job but only by the arrival of the Alaskan winter, in September. All four children were grown, I had been divorced years before, and I had saved enough money to last for more than a year. I was truly free.

I started planning the route in detail, using three main sources: *Exploring Alaska and British Columbia*, by Stephen Hilson, *Coast Pilot #8*, from the NOAA, and the map of the Tongass Forest that showed the 50 sea-level Forest Service cabins.

During those next weeks I reserved and paid for cabins where I could stay for 10 nights of the 80-plus days the trip would require. I mailed some of my gear to friends in Ketchikan, the capable Castle family. Each evening, as I drove the 30 miles home from the job, out through the traffic from the Federal Building in Honolulu, down through the pineapple and sugar cane fields, I planned the evening's work. I dried food and packed it, along with the charts and maps, using a separate box for each segment of the route, then mailed these resupply boxes to myself at five post offices that I had never seen – Ketchikan, Craig, Kake, Sitka, Gustavus. On each box was a note: "Postmaster, please hold for paddling expedition to arrive approximately (date)."

I added hours on the job, preparing for my replacement. I packed away the chaos at the old beachfront home, making it ready for a summer tenant, the rent paying my plane fare. I made copies of the daily route, one for family and one for the Castles, so they'd know where to start a search if I didn't check in along the way. Every detail was taken care of, down to the pencil that had one-inch notches on one side to measure a mile on the topo maps, and notches on the other side to measure a nautical mile on some of the ocean charts.

On a Friday in June, I cleaned my desk and walked out of the office. All was ready. At 11:00 that night I was on the plane heading north.

Adventure. The word is ad-venture, to venture toward. No big declarations of peril, challenge, daring, conquest. No guarantee of making it. Just trying toward.

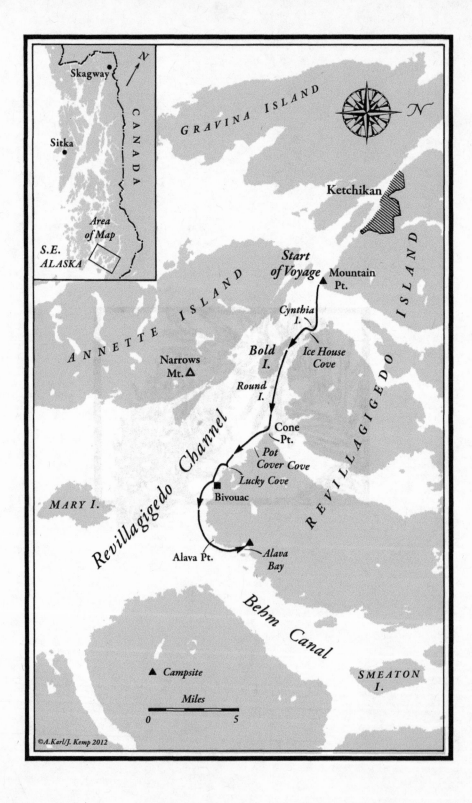

S.E. ALASKA

Skagway

Sitka

CANADA

Area of Map

N

GRAVINA ISLAND

Ketchikan

N

ANNETTE ISLAND

Start of Voyage

Mountain Pt.

Cynthia I.

Bold I.

Ice House Cove

Narrows Mt. △

Round I.

Cone Pt.

REVILLAGIGEDO ISLAND

Pot Cover Cove

Lucky Cove

Bivouac ■

MARY I.

Revillagigedo Channel

Alava Pt.

Alava Bay △

Behm Canal

SMEATON I.

▲ Campsite

Miles

0   5

©A.Karl/J.Kemp 2012

SURVIVAL START

Not until three days after launching was there time enough left from pure survival to even write about my voyage in the journal. Leaving the warmth, good food, and skilled resources of the Castle family's home behind, Mary Castle and I had driven through a rainy Ketchikan, stopping to buy a last-minute frozen steak and the luxury of seven-dollar-a-teaspoon saffron for a future paella dinner.

The plan was to arrive at Mountain Point, south of town, in time to pack and launch on the outgoing tide, southeast down the channel. It was a fine plan that didn't work. In the next few days and more thoroughly all along the trip, I learned that except in tidal narrows, where large bodies of water move back and forth twice each day through a narrow neck, tide is a small factor compared with wind.

"Fair, with occasional light showers," the weather forecast had said, but instead there was solid rain and a strong southeast wind. It was the prevailing wind, southeast 40 percent of the time, my research said, and I was heading into it because I planned to go around Revillagigedo Island counterclockwise for the first leg of the voyage. That way, I could see some of Misty Fjords National Monument, search for the first hot spring, and have a shakedown before crossing the first wide strait. Once across Clarence Strait, I'd hitchhike with the gear and the deflated boat across Prince of Wales Island, pick up my first post office resupply at the small town of Craig, and then paddle north.

In Ketchikan the rain darkened the soil where land and trees had been bulldozed for new houses. Clouds were slung like wet clinging towels across the mountain peaks. Along the two-lane road the ubiquitous pink fireweed was blooming. Fireweed grows near the shores above the Arctic Circle, in Scotland beside Loch Lomond, and in southern Chile. "We call it the Alaskan calendar," Mary said. "The blossoms lowest on the stalk open first, in June, then the bloom moves up the stem through the summer. The last flower at the top catches the first snow."

Timing my progress by the fireweed along the route became one of several recurring themes as I paddled through the months of summer.

Two friends of Mary's and a newspaper reporter were pacing under umbrellas at the boat ramp. Packing my boat while people watch works well after about three weeks, when all has become automatic, but not on the first day, especially now when I was still groggy from the last week's harried work and the plane trip. I needed solo, unpeopled time to think each step through, item by item.

I leashed the double-bladed paddle to the boat by my left knee and tied in the fourth and last waterproof bag, leaving only space to sit with my legs up on top of the bags, my black rubber boots pointing skyward. This was the same comfortable lounge-chair position of so many of my voyages in Hawai'i, but there it had been bare feet or swim fins pointing up. Bare feet were fine in Hawaiian sunshine and 74-degree water. Not here.

I clipped the lifeline harness to the boat by my right hip and took off into the wind without a clear idea of where I was heading. Round Island, the first planned landfall, alternately appeared and disappeared in the rain, but my compass was buried somewhere in a bag. The wind blew me backward while I put on my gloves, which I'd stuffed into a pocket while tying in the gear with bowline knots. At least the knots were automatic. When I teach the kayaking class I warn the students, "You need to be able to tie a bowline upside down, under water, behind your back, holding your breath." I wasn't about to test that ability in this 48-degree water, but above it the knots were easy.

I stroked hard, once every three seconds, out around the tip of Mountain Point. It was my same old swimming-stroke rhythm, one two three, four five six. Before I could afford a boat, and before this one was even manufactured, I used to swim miles of crawl stroke with swim fins along the Na Pali coast of Kaua'i and along the north coast of Moloka'i, towing a bag of gear and camping in the valleys.

A Coast Guard ship was checking buoys in the channel, so I hugged the point until they left, trying to look as if I were just out practicing. I didn't want them to see me heading out to sea and think I needed a rescue, just because there was half a gale and a choppy sea, and what was that silly-looking boat trying to do anyway?

Then I headed southeast. I wasn't aiming for Round Island as planned. I wasn't even heading for the tip of Bold Island, which was two miles closer, but only for the nearest point of land ahead. There were cabins somewhere. I remembered them from the topographic map, but it, too, was down in the gear. I had the nautical chart in a clear plastic bag between my knees, but it showed only the general outline of the land.

Charts are for big boats. They don't need to know the details on the shore, only where it is so they can avoid it. On many charts the first land contour line is 200 feet high, but the shape of the land between sea level and 200 feet is of absolute importance to a paddler for whom land is a refuge, and who has to come ashore each night to camp. We paddlers can't anchor, cook dinner in a warm galley, and climb into a dry bunk. We have to carry the boat up beyond the reach of high tide and create roof, walls, kitchen, and bunk anew each night. We don't care whether the bottom is rock, sand, or mud good for anchoring, only that it's flat and shallow enough to walk ashore and carry up the boat and gear.

It took a hard three-hour paddle to make the two miles to the lee of Cynthia Island up ahead. I could barely make progress against the 15-knot headwind. The seas were choppy and whitecapped. I couldn't stop to rest or I'd go backward. Finally, there was the corner of a building, then the shapes of two small cabins in a sheltered cove. I paddled on into the shallows.

When the boat was fully loaded, its draft was six inches. My rubber boots were 15 inches high. Those nine inches were the margin in which I could step out without either grounding the boat on sharp barnacles or filling my boots with icy water.

After looping the lifeline around a boulder, I checked out the cabins, but they were wet and rotting, with no roofs. In this land where the rainfall is 130 inches a year, corrugated roofs rust and wooden ones rot. Throughout the trip I found that 90 percent of the cabins shown on the old topo maps were already gone.

I paddled on to another cove with 10 intact buildings, three boats, and some skiffs tied to a dock – no people to be seen. I walked up a long ramp from the float looking for a shelter or a place to pitch the tent. Faint music came from a cabin where the door was ajar for a 20-pound cat to come and go. The resident, Pete Ojen, had left his home north of Bergen in Norway to come to Alaska 40 years ago. I had been to Bergen, and reminisced with him. With more time to sit and time to recall, there would have been good stories from 80-year-old, one-eyed Pete, but this meeting was brief. He was wedged into his slat-backed chair, oak solid. His arms were folded; so were the cat's paws. I wondered if I would become a single entity with my boat and paddle, like Pete, cat, and chair. He directed me around the cove to a storage shed with a dry empty area, four by eight feet. It seemed better than searching in the rain for a flat area to rig up tent and tarp.

Outside the cove, the seas were still whitecapped. I went back to the dock and paddled across, unloaded, and hauled up the gear. The tidal life was new and startling: a two-foot orange spined sea cucumber, several new species of starfish, and a small pulsing jellyfish, living together in the clear shallow water with undulating seaweed of green and gold. I noted the high-tide edge of the piled kelp, and tied my boat to a tree well above that line.

The frozen steak was for later; that night's dinner was a quickie of canned spaghetti and cheese, heated on the little Optimus 8R stove. I chinked the slits in the shed wall with moss, inflated the air mattress, and slid into the sleeping bag inside its nylon overbag, and was asleep in 10 seconds. Eleven hours later I woke and grinned. The voyage was under way at last, with the first whole day ahead.

By 9:00 am I was paddling out of the cove. The headwind was down to an estimated 10 knots, but progress was still slow. Over years of paddling I had learned to check my wind speed estimates against a portable wind gauge until my guesses consistently matched the gauge. My thoughts meandered, sprinted, soared, and ceased, in contrast to the steady beat of my paddle. I needed a waterproof tape recorder with a microphone fastened to the foul weather jacket. The body was doing the necessary movements, freeing the mind to float from memory to future and back – free associating, not linear thinking.

One thought: The hazards for an inflatable canoe are greater in occupied places. The docks have nails, frayed rusty cables are just under the surface, and jagged metal pipes lie on the bottom in shallow water. The barnacles and rocks of uninhabited shores are more predictable.

Half an hour pause for lunch, and for what I called a pit stop: dig a pit, defecate, cover it, and wonder why cats but few other animals dig holes. Do lions and tigers? Maybe the powerful cats don't need to cover their scent. No one preys on them. Then power paddle again.

Line up the dark shape of Round Island against the lighter blue of Middy Point five miles beyond; move the island mound across Narrows Mountain to close the gap with Bold Island. The wind was increasing. A wave broke on the bow, throwing solid water over my head, and I paddled hard for the lee of Cone Island, then into the channel between it and the headland. I was pointing into a funnel and moving backward. Making a U-turn, I looked for a campsite north of Cone Point, but the shores were steep, rocky, and overgrown. These weren't *woods*, a word that implies that you can walk along through the trees, nor *jungle*, which seems tropical. Maybe just southeastern Alaska shoreline forest, with its dense tangle of 100-foot-tall spruce and hemlock trees, fallen branches, brush, spiny devil's club bushes, and moss. I paddled close in for half a mile and found no landing place.

Back into the channel. The wind had dropped, so I kept on. I had feathered the blades of the double kayak paddle, keeping them at right angles to each other. That way, as each one moved through the water, the other one was slicing through the air, parallel to it. This meant moving my right wrist up and down, full flex, for each stroke, but it was the most efficient way. If ever I had a tailwind, I would leave the blades parallel to each other, in order to get a small push from the wind as each blade rose for the recovery swing.

Good coves were visible now, but Lucky Cove, still ahead, was marked on my map – a named destination, at least.

Soon I would come to realize that tidal flats on the chart meant a long haul carrying gear, as I could seldom both land and take off on a high tide with a neat 13 hours between the two highs. Tomorrow there would be a range of 23.1 feet between high and low. That vertical range sometimes meant walking a quarter mile over slippery rocks or through sucking mud to get from a low tide landing to a level where the next high water wouldn't quite lick my toes as I slept.

Lucky Cove was that kind of poor choice, but it was 7:30 pm and I'd been paddling nine hours. Farther along in the trip, I learned to trust my intuition to tell me where to camp.

"This one?" the left brain would ask.

"No, two more coves ahead," the right brain would reply.

I found a flat place back in the trees and set up the tent, then carried the gear. I was wet and cold from the waist down. The jacket had kept water off my head and chest, but rain and spray had drained from my boots, which were up on the gunwales, and seeped up my thighs. I changed into dry wool pants, ate cheese and fruit, and went to bed, my outer clothes stacked beside me. That pile of bear scat by the shore was not reassuring. Or was it moose? I didn't yet know.

By 2:00 am I was awake and cold and wet. The tent was a new one and I had not known it needed seam sealant before use – another instance of not putting the gear to the test before an expedition. The rain had dripped steadily through the seams, so the bag was in a puddle and the pile of clothes was sopping. I needed a cabin, and the first one, at Alava Bay, was six more miles.

Lucky Cove was calm, so at dawn I headed out, but within a mile the wind picked up to 20 knots. I was paddling my hardest and moving backward. A beach was ahead, but I couldn't get to it. A tiny bay was behind me, but I didn't want to lose a foot of the ground I'd gained. To my left was a narrow slot in the rock cliff, 6 feet wide and 12 feet to the back. I surged in, crashed against a wall, scrambled out, and floated the boat onto a narrow shelf. Holding the boat with one leg against the surge, I unloaded pack by pack, throwing each one up to a ledge higher than my head. I lifted the boat up to the cliff edge, climbed up the toeholds, then carried everything to higher ground.

I'd lost track of high and low tide. I was shivering and drowsy – danger signs. The windchill factor had dropped the effective temperature below freezing, and I was wet besides. Well aware of deaths from hypothermia, I knew I had to get warm, but everything was wet, including the remedy of a warm sleeping bag. I found a flat place out of the wind back in the thick woods on higher ground and put up the tarp for a shelter from the rain, rigged the tent under the tarp, then carried in more of the gear. The boat was tied bow and stern to a huge log well above high tide. I didn't want it blowing away.

I made hot chocolate on the five-inch-square camp stove and gulped it down. Using a small block of fire starter, some dry inner wood from an old stump, and the paper wrapping the steak, I built a fire. The rain came harder, then a lull, then it poured again. I kept the fire going, using Dr. Clifford Straehley's critical mass system. Cliff is a thoracic surgeon in Hawai'i, but his talents go beyond the medical field. Start a small fire, shielding it with your body or a tarp, and then pile the wood up four feet high. The fire below dries out the wood in the middle, and the mass at the top is a rain shelter to keep the rest burning.

I strung a line and smoke-dried most of the gear between rain bursts. A spark burned a hole in the sleeping bag; I patched it before the down puffed out. I found that only the nylon cover of the bag was wet. Why was I carrying a down bag instead of synthetic in this wet country? Because I already owned it, and I never let it get wet again. I sealed the tent seams until the sealant was gone. I dried my long wool underwear and put it back on.

I went out to check the boat. All OK, but the seas were higher and rougher, coming in long swells with their tops breaking, and I estimated the wind speed at 25 knots. I had considered going back to Ketchikan, but now I wasn't going anywhere, only back to the shelter. I inflated the air mattress, propped it against a log under the tarp, and

started the rite of cooking a steak. Cut off a piece of suet, fry it crisp in a hot pan, insert slivers of garlic into the meat, sear it all to a medium rare, slather with butter, salt, and Ponape pepper, and pour a stemmed plastic glass of Monterey Peninsula Winery Petite Sirah. No veggies tonight; my diet was balanced by the week, not the meal. Eat, drink, and be merry, for tomorrow – oops.

Planes went by, boats went by; none were slow and close enough to be looking for me. This was probably just normal southeast Alaska weather. I laughed grimly at my own egocentricity. I had learned years ago that people are too busy taking care of themselves to be concerned about me. "They" don't really care what you look like, how you're dressed, or what you do, as long as you don't interfere with their lives or self-images. They'll give you a five-second glance, then go back to their own affairs. That realization gives you much more freedom.

The tugboats were out there a mile away, dieseling along with a chunkety-chunk throb. The ferries, cruise ships, and fishing boats all had warm dry cabins. No one invited me to share.

By 6:00 pm I was back in bed with an improvised hot water bottle, dry wool socks, dry long underwear, and a dry sleeping bag. That bear scat was only a mile away, but I needed sleep. The food was sealed and packed and hung from a tree away from camp. I had two pots in the tent to bang together in case of strange sounds in the night. I slept 12 hours.

In the morning, I didn't need to go out through the brush to see what the sea was doing. I could hear it clearly and see the tops of the trees, 50 feet above my head, lashing in the wind. After coffee and oatmeal, I started writing in my journal.

On these trips I'm not really alone. We're a trio. The paddler sizes up the conditions and does the physical labor. The critic sits on my shoulder and nags and growls that I'll never make it, and the writer stands back and laughs, trying to put the three of us into the reality of one grubby body, and also into words for the journal that night.

On all of my expeditions I've kept a daily log: not just the sailor's course and weather, but also the thoughts, the small events, the jeering at myself, and some detailed drawings. Long-ago recollections are always distorted. Time empurples the prose, and the only reality is recorded within a day or two. The writer will need to satisfy the gray, fragile lady at age 90, reading her memoirs from these salty pages.

I also evaluated the equipment. A fine-toothed comb might have been able to get the seaweed and moss out of the hook side of the Velcro on the jacket. The foul-weather gear has literally been a lifesaver, keeping wind out and body heat in. Even without the sealant that came with it (which I used on the tent), the jacket and bib pants have functioned well. I sometimes wished for just waist-high pants, though, or else one of those trough/funnel gadgets for females. The Velcro and zipper fly in these pants is of no use except to scratch a crotch, and to let seawater leak in. After breakfast I had to take off the camera, take off the jacket, undo the suspenders, slide down the pants, tie the suspenders in front of my knees, slide down the pile pants, long underwear, and underpants, use the small pit, then reverse the whole process. Yes, the funnel was a good idea, but I'd have to buy new, male underwear and then find my way through four layers of fly fronts. I figured I could make a funnel by buying one of those offset spout half-pints of engine additive at an auto supply store, and cutting it in half on the diagonal.

By midmorning a plan had evolved: Stay here until the seas went down to the level of my morale, which was rising, then launch at high tide. If it's calm enough to paddle back to Ketchikan, I thought, it will be calm enough to go ahead to Alava Bay. I felt suspended, waiting.

Every hour I walked down through the dense forest to the shore to check on the sea. An elegant small animal came loping over the logs. Pointy nose, dark brown, mongoose size and shape, curious about me. Was it a mink? Someday I might become as familiar with the animals of this country as I had been with the gray squirrels and jays of my childhood in the San Bernardino Mountains, but right now they were all new. I did not yet know what I was seeing; I was simply observing it all with the fresh sight of a child, trying to fit it in with bits of other knowledge that I could remember. There was no one to ask and no reference material for a seaweed, a flower, a bird. Like a child, I looked forward to meeting fishermen and local folk just to ask all the stored-up questions. Perhaps this was the best way to go, with constant wonder and delight.

By now, most of the gear was dry and packed. A diver's neoprene wet suit was my final backup for warmth. I had brought it especially for wearing across the long stretches of open sea, where there was the greatest danger of life-threatening hypothermia in a capsize far from land, but it was too clammy and constricting for daily use. It did make good insulation under the sleeping bag.

The air temperature stayed a steady 47 degrees, with alternating rain and gloomy overcast. No sun. At home in Hawai'i, we average four inches of rain a month, but it can all fall in one hour, and then the sun shines again. Here, the eight-inch average rainfall for June is spread out into all-day drizzles.

I prepared lunch and planned for a siesta, outsleeping the weather. In Harvey Manning's book *The Wild Cascades*, a whole chapter is titled " 'Rain Sleep' ... A traveler must be able not only to sleep out the nights, but also must learn how to sleep away the days, perhaps several in a row." Same weather as here.

How much of the shore from here to Alava could I walk at low tide? Perhaps I could lash together a pack frame. My mind was still running full speed, even though the expedition was going nowhere.

I carried lunch out through the route of moss, bogs, fallen trees, and bushes to eat by the shore. As I straddled a log at 2:00 pm, I saw that the wind and sea had calmed. I went back fast and checked the tide book. It would be high at 3:30. Could I break camp and launch by then, when the water would be high over the top of the cliff I'd climbed up yesterday? Urgency: my mind in overdrive.

At 3:15 I placed the boat in a shallow pool that led out to the now quiet depth between the surging points. At 3:30 the gear and paddle were tied in and the boat was afloat. I lifted the lifeline off the rock, looped it over my left shoulder and under my right arm, stepped in, sat, and paddled out. I'm always fearful of a launching where there is any surf or surge; once at sea and paddling, even when it's rough, I'm more confident.

The small islands and the cove before Alava Point looked like some stage set titled Eden Alaska. A knoll reached out and grabbed my shoulder.

"Here. Put a tiny cabin here, and stay and live and watch the sea."

But these sites would be impossible to reach in a southeastern storm. Could the ferocity of the onshore winter storms be judged by the number of drift logs piled on the beach?

I rounded Alava Point and the water turned a pale clear brown on my paddle blades.

"What dyes the water?" the child asked. Later, many people had answers.

"It's the spruce needles."

"It's the tannin from the high muskeg bogs."

"It's cedar water."

The white obelisk of Mary Island lighthouse lay five miles to the southeast. Was it automated, and if so, what happened to the old light keeper's residence? *Lighthouse* is an *œnomel*, a word evoking a whole way of life, geared to a rhythm of light and fog and the four seasons. "Œnomel" a combination of wine (*œnos*) and honey (*mel*) drunk by the ancient Greeks, by derivation means a strong sweet draught as of language or thought. I've come to use it to describe any word that evokes more than just the meaning of the word. *Cabin, candlelight, wine, valiant, poignant, dusk* – all are œnomel words. Phrases, too – *rain on a tin roof, mountain hut, breaking wave.*

This bay was a bald-eagle commune, with eight of them in sight at once: four on the rocks, two wheeling over the water looking for fish, and two in the trees. The year before on a brief trip I had first heard their voices, like rusty gate hinges, but these were intent on food, not song.

More islands appeared ahead to my right. I had loaded bow-heavy for paddling into the wind, and then with a beam wind and now a tailwind it was doubly hard to steer this rudderless boat. The chart indicated a buoy in Alava Bay, and at last the small white dot showed against a dark shore, then the small cabin tucked into the woods. No boat was moored. Yaay! I had reserved the cabin and paid the fee, but I was a day late. After tying the boat to a rock, I carried up the first load. Holding my breath like a kid on Christmas morning, I opened the door into a small cedar room, 12 by 14 feet.

It was a Hansel and Gretel hut, a gingerbread house, a kid's Daniel Boone fortress. A woodstove by Atlanta Stove Works had a cooking oven below and a warming oven above. Cupboards and a counter lined one corner. The other half of the room had built-in bunks on each side. The upper bunks were twin sizes on the top with doubles on the bottom that also served as benches for the table between.

Four loads of gear went into the cabin, and then I carried up the boat, placed it behind the highest drift log, and tied it to a standing tree. Build a fire, read the logbook of previous guests, unpack, lay out all the clothing to dry more thoroughly, check the boardwalk to the cedar outhouse.

There was time now for the precise arrangement of my gear. Time: the luxury of a stand-up shelter, a woodstove, and a 10-mile view to the north. I inflated the air mattress, shook out the sleeping bag to fluff it, and laid them on a top bunk. From there I could see over my toes to the sea out the front window, and out the back window I could see the forest.

The top shelf of the cupboard was for breakfast food, the middle one for lunch, and the bottom shelf for dinners. One hinged glass window opened into a small, screened box outside. It served as the refrigerator with a steady 47 degrees outside while the inside of the cabin rose to 65 from the heat of the small cast-iron stove. The view into the fridge was now satisfactory, with three kinds of wine and four cheeses, a proper larder. The wine had been decanted at home from glass into lightweight plastic bottles, the labels soaked off and reglued onto the new containers.

I kept running out to the front deck, watching the tide go out, seeing a beach emerge, exhaling a long breath of contentment and wonder: I was a woman in love, a child in a fairy tale. The sun lowered to the mountain behind the cabin and shone through a long tunnel of clouds onto the grass, the bay, and the snowcapped range beyond, burnishing them with a patina of lavender gold. It was an old Maxfield Parrish illustration of a Greek myth.

Inside the cabin the woodstove caressed me with its warmth. The Forest Service crews had stacked logs under a lean-to, ready to split, and driftwood littered the high tide line. Behind the door were a sledge and a wedge, an ax and a saw. Later, I raked the ashes out of the stove, scraped the soot from under the oven, and found all the draft and damper systems. The wood was a problem. Hemlock, spruce, and cedar are soft woods with a low BTU count and few coals, so I broke up hard alder branches from the shore. Hardwood Kellogg oak and soft pitchy ponderosa pine were the ones I grew up with. We had finally written with a soapy rag on the sooty ceiling of our mountain cabin, "This happens if you burn pine. Burn oak."

Like the animals that I would come to know, some day I'd be as familiar with these four Alaskan trees that make up 90 percent of the shoreline forest as I had been with the pines, firs, and oaks of California or the coconut, ironwood, and kiawe that I'd used in Hawai'i for 40 years.

Dinner began with four dozen mussels from the rocks out front, steamed with white wine and onion, the broth mopped up with French rolls. I had the entrée of curry with five sideboys and a glass of wine. There was Chinese squash candy for dessert, then a tot of rum, then the winding down toward sleep. The sun had set at 10:30 pm and even now, at midnight, it wasn't yet quite dark.

I climbed up to the top bunk and into the puffy bag. I took off my knit wool cap for the first time in four days. Beneath was a tangled, salty mat of hair, but at least my warm head had helped keep my whole body warm.

The expedition had been through a rough start, but now I was sheltered and dry and safe. I slept: deep and dreamless.

Simple Camp Curry

4 large dried shiitake mushrooms
1 medium onion
1 tablespoon oil
¼ cup curry powder
1 package powdered coconut milk
1 can chicken chunks, shrimp, cubed firm tofu, or fresh-shucked mussels

Soak mushrooms in ½ cup water. Slice caps, discard stems, save water. Chop onion and sauté in oil. Stir in curry powder. Whisk package of powdered coconut milk into 1 cup of water and add to onions. Add shiitake soaking water and the chicken, shrimp, tofu, or mussels. Thicken with mushroom or chicken instant soup packets if needed. Serve over hot cooked rice with sideboys: chopped peanuts, mango chutney, green onions, raisins, beach asparagus, etc. Makes enough for dinner and breakfast for one paddler.

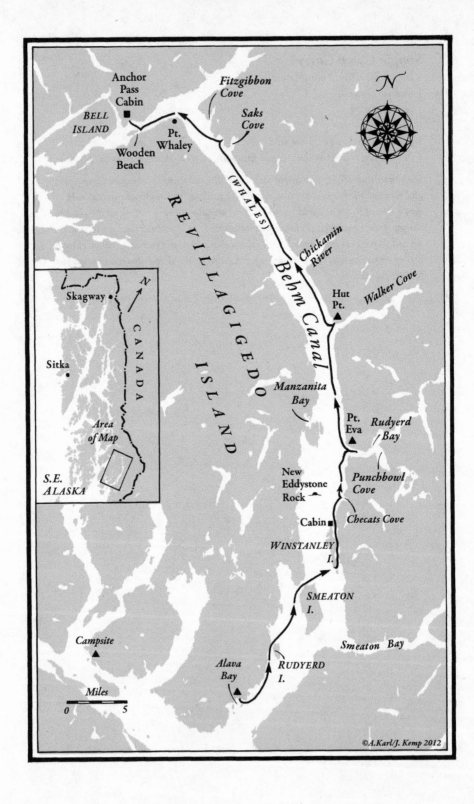

N

Anchor
Pass
Cabin

*Fitzgibbon
Cove*

*Saks
Cove*

BELL
ISLAND

Pt.
Whaley

Wooden
Beach

(WHALES)

R
E
V
I
L
L
A
G
I
G
E
D
O

*Chickamin
River*

Behm Canal

Hut
Pt.

Walker Cove

I
S
L
A
N
D

*Manzanita
Bay*

Pt.
Eva

*Rudyerd
Bay*

New
Eddystone
Rock

*Punchbowl
Cove*

Cabin

Checats Cove

WINSTANLEY
I.

SMEATON
I.

Smeaton Bay

Campsite

*Alava
Bay*

*RUDYERD
I.*

Miles

0   5

Skagway

C
A
N
A
D
A

N

Sitka

*Area
of Map*

S.E.
ALASKA

©A.Karl/J. Kemp 2012

MISTY FJORDS AND WHALES

At three o'clock I woke to the sound of small animals scampering outside. The whole grassy area where I'd landed was underwater; the tide, floating the log at the stern of the boat; was rising to 18 feet, and the sky was getting light.

My body woke again four hours later. It was the body that had needed sleep; all systems and muscles and reactions weary. Now body and mind were both eager for the day in this enchanted wilderness. The tide was ebbing, and I followed it, finding goose tongue plantain for a lunch salad. Wolf tracks were on the sand beach to the north of the cabin. She (all animals are she, in deference to the female of the species, unless proven otherwise) had been there since the dawn high tide. I wondered if she was hungry, if she had cubs, and if I could leave food for her. But if you make friends with a wild animal for your own pleasure and get her accustomed to man, then surely someone will shoot her for his pleasure. As a man in Wrangell later said, "They get too many of our deer." Whose deer?

The resident black bear mentioned in the cabin's log didn't appear, but a deer with soft velvet antlers minced along the beach and up the stream. The cabin was not over-used; only 12 groups in the past year had signed the log. Probably there were more unofficially, fishermen and hunters finding a warm refuge from a storm.

I searched for more alder, the only hardwood available. I was delaying, refiguring. If I could paddle 22 miles tomorrow, I could get to the next cabin, at Winstanley Island, instead of camping on the way. Beyond my route to the northeast was the snowy Rousseau Range. Who had named it, and why for Rousseau? That range was across the border, in Canada, part of a whole continent. Here the scale was to my size, small islands and a small cabin.

In an essay, "The Sea and the Wind that Blows," E. B. White said, "Men who ache all over for tidiness and compactness in their lives often find relief for their pain in the cabin of a 30-foot sailboat at anchor in a sheltered cove." So it was in this cabin ashore. When in my boat, my five cubic feet of gear was compacted into waterproof bags, neat but inaccessible. Here in the 168 square feet of the cabin, those 60 items of gear were sorted into tidy piles with bare wood in between, like the uncluttered interior of a Japanese teahouse. Everything was useful. There were no gewgaws, no desk full of paperwork to be done, and no long list of house repair and maintenance projects. The simplicity was deeply satisfying.

At last the gear was all clean and dry. Now that the voyage was four days along, I reevaluated the necessity of each item, but found I could only eliminate about two pounds. Even that would have to wait two more weeks, until I got to a post office where I could mail it home. I wasn't desperate enough for space to throw it out.

The journal recorded some random thoughts and trepidations:

> *Journal, Day 5: The deer came again. The cabin is 60 degrees, quite comfortable with the sweater and wool pants. As I become more acclimated I'll need less. I'll hug the shore tomorrow, more options and more to see. Will the tailwind hold? It is strange to wake each night and wonder where I am and is this real. At least the boat is holding. Those first two miles it, too, was failing, but it was only an untightened valve.*

After dinner I went out fishing, but found I needed more lessons in the use of the spinning reel. No fish jumped or bit, but it was fine just to sit and absorb the blues and greens of water, sky, and forest as the boat turned slowly through a full circle. Were I to design and create a place for contentment, it would look like this. I came back and partially packed for the morning takeoff.

The mind woke at 1:00 am and said, "Take a look at the 17-foot high tide." Out to the deck in long underwear, T-shirt, and wool socks. The water again was covering the grass, up to the logs. All quiet, with stars. The Dipper was off to the north, its pan upright. Polaris was 55 degrees above the horizon, in contrast to its 21-degree angle in Hawai'i. That measure is the same as your latitude above the equator. In Hawai'i, Polaris is called Hoku Pa'a, "Stuck Star." Cassiopeia was there in the east, and the Pleiades. But something else was there. Lights in the sky. Not dawn, but all the northeastern sky had shapes that moved, emerged, and faded. Patterns formed and changed like clouds blown by the wind. Sometimes they hung in long shreds, sometimes in layers. No color, just every shade of gray, from pearl to deepest ash. A comet with a tail, but filling a quarter of the sky. A pulse to the north, then fading. A searchlight forming to the east, then dimming. I came in and lit a candle, made a cup of hot milk with brown sugar, then put on my jacket and went back out to sit on the stump for another hour, awed at the light show reflected in the water at my feet.

At 6:00 am the stiff paddler woke again, stretched, climbed down from the bunk, and made coffee on the small stove, then built a range fire for warmth and the final drying. A soft-boiled egg, hot roll, oatmeal with brown sugar and milk. More coffee, hot Tang. I packed the gear and loaded stern heavy, hoping for tailwinds, gentle ones. I closed the door and patted my cabin farewell, then launched.

Paddling long stretches in midchannel was tedious, so I hugged the shore, watching the layered zones of the barnacles, mussels, seaweed, and starfish as the rising tide covered the cliffs.

There were other thoughts in the long, autopilot hours of paddling. On this day of high overcast and glare on the water, I pulled the wool cap down low on my forehead, making a fuzzy, thick eyebrow out of the folded edge, then remembered back. Years ago on our own fishing boat out of San Pedro, my husband had worn his old navy watch cap the same way – not jauntily on the back of his head, the way I liked it, with the brown curls escaping onto those high cheekbones, but set square and low like a visor, parallel to the deck and to the far horizon. On this trip I had learned the value of a knit cap, first for whole-body warmth, and now to cut the glare.

I understood better, too, why he went back to fishing in California, leaving me in Hawai'i with the four children. He was a seagoing man, John was, not a good father or husband. After years of Coast Guard duty and two more years of federal jobs in the Pacific Islands, perhaps he needed that one man, one fishing boat time, just as I had needed this solo trip. Years after the divorce – when he had earned his master's license to be the captain of a vessel of any tonnage, on any ocean – he returned to Hawai'i on a brief visit. Another woman had gentled him, had refused, in the newer ways of women, to put up with abuse. I began to like him again, to find an old-new friend, and then he died of lung cancer. I paddled on. It shouldn't have taken so many years to better understand the man I had married too young.

The route was north now, up Behm Canal. The name sounds like a man-made waterway, but Captain George Vancouver called it that in 1793, as he titled others, whose names have changed from "Canal" to "Channel" in the years since.

Up the pass between Rudyerd and Revillagigedo Islands, then across the two miles to Smeaton Island in a 20-knot wind. A red powerboat, the *Sweet Thunder*, slowed and came toward me. I waved that I was OK, though steering with the wind and seas on the stern quarter was hard. They throttled up with a sound to match the name and headed on south. Throughout the whole trip, no one at 50 yards would know I was a woman: The wool cap hiding the blond hair and the foul-weather jacket were bulky disguises.

It was tricky paddling through the troughs. If by mistake I slid a paddle into the water on the downwind side, with the blade flat against the boat, just as a sea lifted the upwind side, it could mean an instant pole vault and upsy over.

The boat, boots and clothing, 60 pounds of gear, and a cap over my ears made too many layers between body and water. They separated the animal senses from the pulse of the sea. The less gear between me and the sea, the better I was able to sense the sea's movements and respond. Swimming around cliffs, as I had on Moloka'i years before, landing bare body onto rocks, it was easier to be part of the elements. Even paddling, clad in a bikini and with the warm Hawaiian seas splashing on my shoulders, I could feel the boat as part of my hips and swing in a hula motion through a passage in the reef.

Winstanley cabin, 10 miles ahead, was still the goal, but it was late and raining. Around the north end of Smeaton Island I looked for a campsite, but there were only bogs where it was flat, and the rest of it was thickly overgrown and blocked by rows of half-floating, tangled drift logs, an indicator of fierce northern outflow winds. North and southeast seemed to be the only wind directions. Not until nine years later, at the base of the high ridge of Dall Island, did I learn about the swirling williwaws, which

blew from all the compass points to flatten me from overhead. Here there was no place both flat and bare enough to pitch a tarp or tent, and it would take an hour with hatchet and saw to create one.

It was 7:40 pm. The seas were running north, and I calculated the risks of waves and darkness. I noted the compass course, 60 degrees, in case Winstanley Island ahead disappeared in the rain. It did, but the compass and the wave angle both showed the direction.

On the southern tip of the island, an hour later, the terrain changed to grassy clearings between forested points. In one meadow were two geese. They resembled our Hawaiian goose, the nene, the same taupe body and black head, but these had a white throat and cheek. A naturalist once said, "In all the world of animals, it would be hard to improve on the Canada goose." One of their attributes was that they were thought to be monogamous, mating for life. "Until death do us part" might be true for them, I thought; it's less often true for my species. Later I found it had proved untrue for Canada geese as well. The geese probably value wisdom, too, since they take turns leading the flock and drafting – following with a slight windbreak from the one just ahead and at an angle: the wisdom of the V-formation. Then there's the uncanny ability to find their way back home after the long flight south for the winter. Later, I learned that most of the geese in southeastern Alaska are nonmigratory.

Throughout the voyage I would hear the sound of wild geese as flocks flew over. They say geese honk. That isn't the right word. It isn't an *ooga* like a Model A Ford, or a *beep* like a VW. It's a symphony of a dozen clear trumpets and haunting French horns all on different notes. It's Circe and the Lorelei and a lonely, ancient train whistle. All the poems and clichéd country songs are true.

Paddling on through Shoalwater Pass, I knew I'd make it: 22 miles in 10 hours. This slow boat would probably not exceed that mileage until I went through the Sergius Narrows a month later on a full nine-knot ebbing tide, with a tailwind.

Ahead lay a buoy – and a boat and people on shore by the cabin: three adults and three kids. My preference for solitude was balanced by their hospitality. In the morning, 12-year-old Rick taught me fishing techniques for the spinning reel and confirmed that I had been seeing mink.

It was quiet and bare when they left. Overcast, and the wind had shifted to the north: a headwind again. Time was almost palpable here. No jangling distractions, no unpredictable sounds, simply the cabin, my gear, and the natural elements. I stood on the deck, leaning on the rail: receiving. A woodpecker hammered on a distant tree. A river otter swam across from the round island in the bay, cleaving the water with a miniature bow wave and a wake behind. Is the angle of the wake the same for a fast boat as it is for a loon or an otter? She came ashore, twitched her brown nose, and humped her way up the gravel-and–barnacle shell beach into the grass. Across the water, hidden in the forest, a grouse was drumming. An hour went by so slowly that it seemed a whole day of peace had passed.

I picked up the water bag and walked the winding path to the stream. Even off the trail, the woods here were almost walkable, and if there was sun it would filter through to the moss carpet. Most of the southeast Alaska shores are such places of texture. Underfoot is the duff in the forest, the bog mud on the trails, the shale and sand on shore, and fucus seaweed on the rocks. The bark of the hemlocks is stringy, ropy, and the trunks are like heavy twisted hawsers. Spruce is darker, and scaly. This old forest with its big trees is saved from logging by being part of the Misty Fjords National Monument. A spruce here is 15 feet around, and huge fallen trees become nurse logs, with young trees sprouting in a line from their lengths. I planned to set a crab net that night – any excuse to stay longer.

This cabin had a small Fireview heating stove, not a cooking range. There were only two platelets for cooking, but it held the heat well and used very little wood. A passion for woodstoves is ingrained. From age eight I grew up cooking on one in our mountain cabin. I pat and pet and feed one like a new cat friend until we're both purring, it with the vibration of hot flames and me with warm bliss.

By afternoon half the sky was sunshine, and the cabin temperature was up to 65 degrees without a fire. I knew that all this was pure decadence for a real Alaskan, and remembered reading in Billie Wright's *Four Seasons North* how she and her husband up in the Brooks Range in winter found it positively balmy when the thermometer rose to zero.

Policing the yard, picking up cans, gum wrappers, and cigarette butts, I suddenly smiled at a remembrance. Once, in Hawai'i, I was holed up in a mountain cabin next to one where Gregory Bateson, author of *Steps To An Ecology of Mind*, was writing. In the evenings we sometimes met on walks. He was a chain-smoker, lighting a new one from the last, but he mashed out the butt, shredded and scattered the tobacco, and carefully put the paper and filter in his pocket. More than all his brilliant writing, I remember that small demonstration of an ecology of the mind.

When the tide was at its lowest I laid my nylon net hammock flat on shore, tied the ends to big rocks, and baited it with smashed mussels. Four blue herons waded ashore in the golden light. From the top of a bare old spruce an eagle went through his repertoire, a harsh cascade of notes like a mezzo-soprano with a sore throat caroling down the scale, the jangled song of wilderness I'd been waiting for all year.

Journal, Day 8: Sunshine! Every kitchen should have the morning sun flooding in through an east window (and have a small symbolic drawing of a dragon hunched over it for the protection of the house, say my Chinese friends). Climb down from the top bunk. Pull on the jacket and pants. Put on the water for coffee. Go to the outhouse. Run back along the trail, the soft duff underfoot, remembering the 10-year-old self racing down a yellow pine needled trail at Barton Flats in California. Put the

bowl of steaming oatmeal on the front deck rail. In a bent knee, thigh
stretching second ballet position it's just the right height.

I checked the crab net. Bait gone, no crabs. I reread the cabin logbook. "Kushtaka in the bay," said a group from Anchorage. Is that a seal? So much to learn. The water is fresh and fragrant like wine. Winstanley Creek Winery. The grape is spruce needle, Vintage 1981. Color pale amber. Clarity excellent. Taste demi-sec.

At nine o'clock I left the cabin and paddled north. Two miles away on the topo map was Checats Cove, with the alluring symbol and the word *Cabin*. No cabin was there, only remains, but back in the deep tangled shade were two marble headstones. "Old Checat, Died Sept 27, 1901, Age 89" and "Steargh Glah, Died Sept 27, 1901, Age 76." What was the story of their same-day deaths and of their lives? Were they a Tlingit chief and his wife? I asked their permission for a photo and said I came in humility with a wish to know and understand, then quietly left them there in the shadows. I forgot to ask them about Kushtaka. Later I found the answer to my question about the death of Checat and Steargh Glah in Patricia Roppel's book *Southeast Alaska's Panhandle*: They were two Tlingit men fighting over fishing rights to a stream. In another source, I found that Kushtaka was a creature in an old Tlingit legend, half man, half otter, who terrifies little children.

When I returned, my boat was stranded by an ebbing tide, so without unloading it I lifted one end and then the other, zigzag, sliding on the kelp, back to deep water, and went on. Out to the left in the center of Behm Canal was New Eddystone Rock, a shaft 230 feet high, named by Vancouver in 1793 for its resemblance to the lighthouse rock off Plymouth, England. Ahead to the east was the mile-wide entrance to Rudyerd Bay. I had run off the B-3 quadrangle topographic map and was now on Ketchikan C-3. All of those brown contour lines so close together meant one thing: cliffs.

Day by day I was becoming part of this world. With no other human to communicate with, I began to forget I was human. I felt I was part of the sea and the animal world. Ahead on the rocks was a lustrous brown mink at the water's edge, so engrossed in prying loose a mussel that she did not see me. I floated quietly, 15 feet away, taking photos. She looked up, gave a happy chirp, dived into the water and swam out to meet me, both of us with a grin of welcome. Just beside my boat she suddenly saw me up close and looked around in horror. She did a U-turn dive, swam underwater to the rock shore and raced across the mussels and granite to the edge of the trees, then paused and looked back.

"Hey, it's OK. I'm just your Auntie Audrey from Hawai'i," I chittered. She disappeared, but perhaps she still watched from hiding. For a few moments there had seemed to be a communication, one water animal to another.

I paddled on, laughing, into Rudyerd Bay, noting sheer cliffs ahead and the wall to my right, laced with intrusive sills and dikes of darker granite, realizing also that I was looking at spots that were limpets, clinging to the smooth rock. In the Hawaiian language they are 'opihi, a delicacy to be pried off, gouged out of the shell, and eaten raw, chewier and sweeter than an oyster. But they occur worldwide, so I've made them into chowder in Portugal, simmered them in butter and garlic like escargot in France, and put them into a rice dish in Palau. I stopped and pried off enough for supper.

On into the fjord: a 3,000-foot-high headland to the left, a 2,500-foot slope to the right. I turned into Punchbowl Cove. That long curved dome across the cove had a familiar look. Like Yosemite and the whole of southeastern Alaska, this place had been shaped by glaciers that rounded the peaks and scoured the valleys, like a giant adze in the hands of a master carpenter. *The Guinness Book of Records* says that my old paddling area of north Moloka'i in Hawai'i has the highest sea cliffs in the world. This dome is as high as those, and in New Zealand's Milford Sound there are ones higher still, but in both places they are the result of glacial action carving a fjord, not the sea itself and the wind-borne rain lashing and eroding the cliffs. New evidence shows that a series of giant submarine landslides helped form the north- and east-shore cliffs of Moloka'i.

It would be six more miles to get to the head of Rudyerd Bay, a full day in and back out. I swung the boat in a full circle, trying to etch the scene on my bones, then reversed the route out to the north corner of the bay entrance and landed at high tide on a small pebble beach between two angled dead trees.

I walked around the site, incredulous. I was a real estate agent showing the property. "You have a natural wood counter (a fallen tree) here in the kitchen with a sunset view. The stream water supply is especially pure and clean. Back here to the left is the bedroom. Note the woodland scene on the wallpaper on three sides, with a seascape on the fourth, and do appreciate the moss green carpeting with six inches of resilient foam underneath. To the right is the bathing room. Our waterfall showerhead is the hard-massage type, not a water saver. The temperature is set on summertime heat saver."

By sundown I was delirious. It had been a whole day of sunshine. There were to be only five more out of the 85 days of the voyage. I sat naked on a smooth rock after a swim in the ocean, 46 degrees, and a dip under the waterfall, 38 degrees, and four dozen steamed limpets swirled in garlic butter. I sipped minted hot chocolate while watching the light of sunset gilding the colors of a blue sea, brown mottled tree bark, and the gleaming pink pebbles. Across the two-mile width of Behm Canal were the snowy ridges of Revillagigedo Island.

In Hawai'i that golden time lasts only a few minutes. Paddling in the tropics, you had better be where you're going by sunset, because it will be dark in half an hour. Here the sunset goes on and on, hours of shading through gold to rose to mauve.

I climbed into bed, a soufflé of air mattress and down bag on springy moss. Could I possibly endure these wilderness hardships? "I'd rather wake up in the middle of nowhere than in any city on earth" – not John Muir or Thoreau, but Steve McQueen.

I had left the stove just outside the tent, so in the morning, I had only to wiggle on my belly a foot to the door to make coffee. I drank it propped on my elbows, admiring the view, while still in my sleeping bag. Colin Fletcher had his tea that way on his walk through the Grand Canyon, and perhaps Robert Louis Stevenson before him, who wrote of traveling with a donkey in the Cevennes, had tea from his Primus while still in his sleeping bag. I thought I should like to do that journey without the donkey, or perhaps paddle some of the rivers of France, connecting castles and wineries instead of campsites and waterfalls. So in 1994, I did paddle this same French-made Sevylor boat model down the Loire, camping on islands in the stream. In 2001, I paddled down the Vezere in southwest France, lunching on Brie and good French bread at the base of castle walls. Stevenson canoed a more northern French river, and his *An Inland Voyage,* published in 1878, like this book, is often an account of paddling in the rain. Both of Stevenson's journeys lasted less than two weeks. Mine would be 12. We both sought man-made shelters when we could.

A ship came up the channel and turned in to the bay. I leaped for the binoculars and saw a hammer and sickle on the stack, and the name *Odessa.* A Russian cruise ship! She must have gone all the way to the back of the fjord, as it was two hours before she returned. Could I have paddled out to greet her passengers? How many kayakers are there in Russia? Another paddling book could be written about voyaging down the Volga River to the Black Sea, but how many dams, hazards to a paddler, are on the Volga? The Loire in France is 650 miles with no dams. Chile, with its seacoast of fjords and an inside passage, is another ambition.

I figured that if I made the 12 miles to Hut Point and took a look at Walker Cove all in one day, I'd be back on schedule. Schedules! I did it to myself. Nothing said I had to meet those dates but my own parsimony, not wanting to waste the money I'd paid for a cabin.

By nine o'clock I had packed and launched, making a final spin to look back at the home I was leaving. A tailwind picked up in the afternoon, and I took fast photos as I crossed the mouth of Walker Cove fjord, then drove ashore at Hut Point in a hard chop, swinging between the sharp edges of the mussel-covered boulders.

On the topo map, an empty square was marked, denoting an abandoned building on one of the small islands off the point. I crisscrossed the islet, finding no evidence of one, but on the point of land nearest the islands were the remains of a cabin, logs notched at the corners. John Graves, in one of my top 10 books, *Goodbye to a River,* has some comments on the effective ways to notch log cabin corners. But it isn't the corners, it's the roof that is crucial wherever there are heavy rains. Once it leaks, whether with rain or melting snow, everything else rots, the roof collapses, and in a few years there are only humps of moss-covered logs and boards and rusty scraps of a woodstove.

But a campsite was there at Hut Point, waiting – a flat patch of grass above high tide, a small stream, wild lupine and shooting-star flowers, and a mossy spot for the tent. Dinner was a sour-cream noodle Stroganoff with goose-tongue salad. The wine was Hut Creek Winery white.

I was camped on the mainland here, a part of the whole continent, not on an island. That increased the likelihood of one more hazard. Grizzly bears. From the time I'd first visited Alaska two years before, bear stories had been dinned into my head. Now the first line of the Alaska Department of Fish and Game brochure leaped out of that corner where it had been lurking; "Alaska is bear country and you're in it." It went on to say that actually the probability of being injured by a bear was only one-fiftieth that of being injured on the highway. That's what I tell people about sharks in Hawai'i, but it was small consolation here, 70 miles from the nearest road.

"But didn't you have a gun?" people will say.

No. A gun big enough to have any effect on a 500-pound bear would weigh between 5 and 10 pounds. I'd need to have it on my hip every moment. Ammunition would weigh another 5 pounds. I didn't have room for that weight and bulk in a nine-foot boat. I would need to clean and oil a gun every day to keep it clear of salt and rust, and I doubted the ability of any gun I could carry on my hip to stop a charging bear. A wounded bear would be even worse. Coexistence was preferable. I was to experience grizzly bears and black bears later, from two feet away. But not here.

Away next morning on another sunny day, and soon I was paddling in shirtsleeves, with Behm Canal like a quiet lake. Lupine blossoms were tucked into the lines on the bow: a bit of bravado. The color film supply was getting low, so I had loaded with black-and-white. Today I was supposed to find the first hot spring. I passed the Channel Islands and then the Chickamin River, checking the map closely, noting each symbol for a freshwater spring.

Suddenly there was a big water sound ahead. It was not the sound of a salmon jumping. It was not a seal spotting me and doing an instant up-and-over dive. This was a huge volume of water. Coming toward me were two whales, heading south down the channel. Not the humpbacks that I knew from Hawai'i, these were pure black, with a high narrow dorsal fin and a 10-foot span between spout and fin. Killer whales! I spun away and paddled fast toward the cliff, but there was no place to get ashore. The critic on my shoulder scolded the yellow-bellied paddler. "You don't have to carry the yellow color scheme that far." I turned and stroked parallel to them, but they had already passed.

Disappointed, I turned back to the search for a hot spring. Five miles south of Saks Cove, said the USGS thermal springs book, and 200 feet inland. I came to a cove and landed. The major stream was farther south than the map indicated, but I found a smaller one that seemed possible, of a size that might have bubbled from just one spring. Its water was icy, but it would chill fast on this ground, so I crawled upstream, through the spiny devil's club, under logs, through the water. Finally I stopped; 300 feet in half an hour. No steaming vapor showed ahead, no sign of the red algae that often grows near hot springs. I had no assurance a hot spring was still bubbling. The

Geological Survey report was from a 1917 observation, and the 1980 NOAA report on hot springs of Alaska didn't mention it. Until further reconnaissance, it will remain a mystery. I paddled on.

Again I heard the big water sound, like the steam jets on a locomotive. Two whales were moving north. More were coming. I stopped paddling, waiting. The critic had shamed the paddler into not fleeing. One whale lifted higher, and I could see the white undermarkings: orca, the killer whale, unmistakably. A single one angled off from the pod toward me, dove, then surfaced 200 feet away. He blew once, a misty cloud, then dove again, leaving ruffles of white water on the surface. He rose again, 100 feet away, still on course toward me, the spray from his blowhole and the dorsal fin both in a line, aimed like an arrow toward my boat. The fin was five feet high, firm and erect. A young male, I thought, a maverick, curious and unpredictable in the way of teenagers everywhere. I measured: "Two hundred, one hundred... hmmm."

In quick motions, I dipped the paddle once on each side to make sure his sonar knew my precise location, then laid the paddle down and waited, camera to my eye, all heartbeat and adrenalin. A surge; the boat lifted. He surfaced across the bow, five feet in front of the boat, lifted it with his own bow wave, brushed it in his arc, blew air and water. Was there an eye looking at me? I saw him only through the camera lens and pressed the shutter as the huge bulk rose and went down. I was gasping. The droplets on my arms were from his wet breath. Male? Female? I wasn't certain, though the dorsal fin seemed to be five feet high, so that would be a male. In those days before orca sightings and studies were frequent, I'd seen what an orca naturalist would have given five years of life to see. Dazzled, bewitched, and so lucky to have been there. Orcas are in the dolphin family, and many people find a special communication between man and dolphin. Had he seen the yellow boat from a distance and been curious? I don't know. Their diet is fish and sea mammals. Am I a sea mammal?

Recently orca specialists have suggested that the returning sonar sound from my inflatable craft would seem to an orca more like the ping of a seal's body than the sound from a hard-shelled boat. I'm not sure I want that piece of information.

In 2002, Alexandra Morton's excellent *Listening to Whales* was published by Ballantine Books. She tells of the fish diet of the resident orcas in the area between northern Vancouver Island and the British Columbia mainland. The orcas of the transient population ate seals and porpoises. What is the preferred food of these orcas of southern Alaska? Are they the same group as in B.C.?

I paddled on, looking for a campsite. With this quiet water I should have crossed the channel, which I'd have to do soon, but I was tired and my right arm was aching. I passed Saks Cove: fifteen miles today. The wind came up, and I stopped at the Geological Survey mark for Joy, as the map called the site. I learned later that I should have gone to Fitzgibbon Cove.

It wasn't a joyous campsite, but it was adequate. Camp requirements:

1. *A shore I can get the boat up, not a sheer cliff.*

2. *A place above high tide, level and clear enough for the tent.*

3. *Protection from the wind, as windblown rain blasts under tarps and sneaks into tents.*

4. *Space to rig and tie the nylon tarp rain shelter overhead so I can cook, dress, and pack outside of the three-foot-high tent but also out of the rain.*

Those are the necessities. Then come the niceties: a stream to make music through the night and supply more water than the minimum two quarts I carry; wild flowers; a sunset view or morning sun warmth (it's rare you can get both); some old driftwood boards to make a counter and a table; a tree to hang things on; a crosscut section of driftwood log for a stool; a supply of mussels; a smooth beach free of barnacles for landing and launching; and a place to dive into the sea if the sun is really warm. Sometimes, also, an intangible something that feels like home. This place had only the first four, the necessities, but it would do.

Years ago, in a university class in counseling, I took a Strong-Campbell Interest Inventory and found that my highest single score was in domestic arts. That was puzzling, because aside from a delight in creative cooking I wasn't much of a housekeeper. Then one day the lightbulb flashed overhead, as in the comic strips. It was the nest-building instinct that had skewed the score: I had an overwhelming passion for creating a small place to live that suited all the senses. As children, my cousin Sid and I had built tree houses, gunnysack tepees, cowboy shacks for broomstick horses, and I still delighted in small cabins. At home I have a collection of books about tiny houses. My next-highest scores were nature, science, mechanics, and adventure. Here on this expedition I used all of those interests every day. Probably that's why I kept coming back to this country, every year for the next 20 years. It fit me, I fit it.

At dawn the wind was up: whitecaps and choppy seas. Two miles to cross the channel, but that would be right in the troughs. Four miles to Point Whaley if I angled, and I had to angle; the troughs were too dangerous.

The paddler embarked, but the critic carped, "Can you embark in an inflatable canoe, or does it have to be a bark canoe, or is it only in a bark or barkentine you can embark? Anyway, shove off."

I had an incoming tide, 11.7 feet at 10:00 am; this wasn't the 20-foot range between high and low of a week ago. The chart said tide rips. The chart was correct. Rips, troughs, and curling seas, and the boat slewing off the crests. It was my first experience with the stubby six-by-six-by-six waves of Alaska's Inside Passage: six feet high, six feet thick, and six feet between. Those proportions were perfect for bouncing each end of a nine-foot boat in a different direction. I kept thinking a week ahead to the eight-mile crossing of Clarence Strait. What if the wind and seas were like this!

By ten o'clock I was across to Whaley Point, but it was as tough a four miles as I had ever done. The tides up and down both sides of the 60-mile-long Revillagigedo Island meet and part here, and the Unuk River current comes in from the northeast. Tide against current and wind causes rips and rough seas, a fact I was to learn thoroughly outside Baranof Island in 1985, and in Smith Sound in British Columbia in 1988, and across lower Behm Canal in 2002.

Soon came my reward: the first loon – with an unexpected grace in its arched neck. I'd only seen photos. Involuntarily my hand moved off the paddle shaft into an arc of imitation. She paddled away, caroling her song. Some people hear the loon's call as a crazy laugh; it doesn't sound like that at all to me. Other people have made comments indicating a certain compatibility between this voyage and loons. That's fine by me. "Crazy as a loon."

On the shore ahead was the greatest mass of drift logs of the whole trip. Down the great Unuk River they come, toppled, uprooted, carried by the torrents of the melting snows. The currents and winds carry them here, where they smash ashore, shatter, and pile entwined in a giant's game of jackstraws. There was no way to haul a boat and loads of gear across, although it is a narrow neck and would have saved me a mile of paddling. As I stepped out to explore, the boat floated onto soft turf made of thousands of soaked bits of bark and chips. A wooden beach!

I tied the boat, then clambered through the tunnels of logs to walk the long dry boles, up, down, and over the obstacle course to an isthmus of emerald grass and blue iris. Certainly there was an endless supply of firewood and building lumber here. I needed to learn how to operate the Alaskan mill, a portable chain saw in a jig, used to cut timber into planks. The local residents often cruise the shore, looking for logs of the species they want, usually cedar, then tow them home behind their boats. They don't have to saw to two-by-four or other standard sizes; they saw to suit the project – whatever fits.

I paddled back around Claude Point and on to the reserved Anchor Pass cabin. No one was there. Good thing: Tired, I would have been churlish and crotchety. Welcoming hospitality would come later.

Limpets, or ʻopihi (patelles in French)

Pry them off the rocks by slipping a knife blade between the shell and rock. Be quick, before you touch them and they clinch down. Put them face down into a pan of melted butter and chopped garlic. Simmer until they release from their shells.

Or,

Place face up on a one-inch spaced grill. Blop with butter and minced garlic. Cook over the coals until they slide loose from their shells. Hawaiian plus French equals ʻopihi escargots.

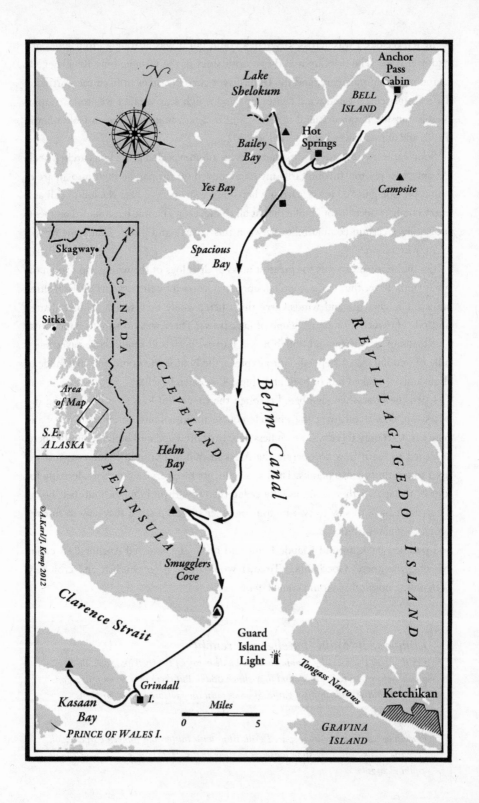

CABINS AND CLARENCE STRAIT

The pattern: Tie up the boat, stand quietly and listen for clues to this new place, then carry up a load of gear, lift the latch to my new home, and check the stove. This cabin at Anchor Pass had a sheepherder stove, an oblong box without an oven. In Maine they call it a chunk stove. A long wet walk led through high beach grass to the stream, but all else was luxurious.

At three o'clock I arrived, and by six had washed and dried the wool underwear and socks and was creating an elegant Japanese dinner. I patted and rolled, simmered and fried, thinking of other Asian dinners. Years before, on business trips to Japan, I had learned what could be done with rice and bits of fish. The artisan sushi makers, after long apprenticeship, become so deft as to make a ritualistic, delicate ballet of the movements of fingers, palms, and wrists in shaping each two-inch block of rice. Index and middle fingers of the right hand pat the blob in the left palm. Left wrist twists the rice a quarter turn, fingers pat again until the shape emerges. I got churned up watching it, like the gut reaction to seeing a wet clay bowl growing in the hands of a master potter at the wheel. The final shape is a bite-size loaf, topped with a translucent layer of raw fish, shrimp, urchin roe, or any of a dozen other delicacies. At home I had a poster of sushi with color photos of all the different kinds, and the names in Japanese and in English.

Here, I made do with ingredients from the shore and in my food sack, then laid it all out on a red-bandanna place mat. First the hot wet *oshibori* washcloth, then hot sake to sip, sushi rolled in black nori seaweed, miso soup, a mound of hot rice, a tempura assortment of fresh mussels, rehydrated mushrooms, and fucus seaweed, and finally smoked oysters from a can.

There was even powdered and moistened wasabi for dipping the sushi. You had to be cautious with that, if you wanted to keep the top of your head intact. There was a mug of tea, and a sweetened black-bean paste for dessert. I surveyed it all.

"Hah." I ran out to whittle chopsticks from spruce twigs. Next time, I'll bring a pack of *hashi* from Hawai'i. Those dry white pine sticks would make fine kindling.

After dinner it was time for a bath, but there was no *furo*, no traditional Japanese bath, to go with the dinner theme. Before commercial shower bags were available, I had combined the lining of a five-liter wine box with a tube and a rubber sink-faucet spray nozzle. It could be filled with hot water, placed inside the nylon bag I'd sewn at home, and hung shoulder high from a tree. The bag had a corner hole for Summit wine and a center hole for Franzia. But standing naked in the chill air, I didn't want little sprays of water on one side while I froze on the other. I needed to soap quickly, then have a big slosh of water. I filled my large pot to the brim, heated it on the woodstove to elbow comfort, soaped, then hooked in the detachable handle and stepped out onto the deck. A big dumped wash of the warm water, then back inside to rub down the shivers and dry by the stove.

> *Journal, Day 12: Anchor Pass Cabin. Dug out the postcards. Ah yes. That was Orca for sure. I have a fine picture on a card. How will my own photo come out? At least seven were in that pod, maybe more, and all different sizes. A half-mile spread between the first two, my curious one, and the last four. Were the first two scouts and were they the same ones returning to the pod that I first saw heading down the channel?*

Some basic decisions in the outhouse this morning: The ominous thought of crossing Clarence Strait was always there. The NOAA *Coast Pilot #8* says of Clarence, "Current has a maximum velocity of four knots and strong southeasterlies" and "...gales may blow down the strait from the NW." I had never before crossed eight miles of open sea. But one basic decision I made was "Start worrying less and enjoying more: 'Tis a mad spoof of an expedition, to be sure."

Back to the cabin. The skylight panels of corrugated plastic were great for letting in light, but there under the trees, the drip and falling twigs were amplified into a constant *ping, pung, thump, crack, poing*. Scientists have said that drops of water from trees are larger than open-sky raindrops; the water slides toward the needle or leaf tip and hangs there until the weight overcomes the surface tension. T. J. Walker, author of *Red Salmon, Brown Bear*, called them "accumulation drops."

All day the heavy clouds sat on Anchor Pass and on the 2,400-foot-high unnamed mountain across the way. Gray, lacy mist was tangled in the tops of hemlocks, a gray-green layer of trees and land came down to the shore, gray-blue water reflected the clouds, and in the foreground was the muted-gold fucus on the wet rocks. Smoke from my stove drifted out over the bay. A loon called; an eagle added its rasping cadenza. Minutes passed, then a single clear thread of sound was laid on the air, then one more, a note lower. The two-note song of the varied thrush will forever recall this misty enclosed world.

At one o'clock a 30-foot ketch ghosted along, half a mile away, heading down Behm Narrows, tacking easily from one side to the other with jib, main, and mizzen. After five days alone I was ready for good company, but she went on by. Few sailboats actually raise their sails in southeastern Alaska. The channels are narrow and the winds are fluky. Most boats rely on motors, but these were evidently real sailors.

Teatime: cheese and hot buttered rum tea. The canned Camembert cheese keeps fine without refrigeration. Another culinary note: Grape Kool-Aid plus vodka as a wine cooler just doesn't make it. Better to use each one straight. My homemade jerky is good, too, but of course all Alaskans figure they know the best jerky recipe, starting with "Take one moose..."

No Alaskans were with me, and people will ask, "But weren't you lonely?"

Yes, but it was of my own choosing. I never felt lonely except inside a cabin when it was raining. Then I was a human and sometimes lonely for another good human. Camped out under just a tarp with no walls and with all the wild out there at the four edges, I was a wary animal, alert to every sound, a part of it. If I wanted company I could paddle out and find it somewhere within 50 miles. If I wanted to be a people person, I could do something nice for the next camper who came along, even though we might never meet, like leaving a big supply of dry, split wood and a fire laid in the stove, ready to light. Instead of carving a name on a cabin wall, this kindness had always been my signature and trademark.

The cabins were a delight throughout the trip. In this year's 85 days I would use 11 of them, each then 10 dollars a night. The Forest Service, under the U.S. Department of Agriculture, had the huge job of administrating the whole Tongass National Forest, with all the interwoven interests of logging, fishing, mining, recreation, and people's homes. Despite budget cuts and increasing pressures, it seemed that the individuals were doing their best, even though no one interest group, not even the employees themselves, were ever in agreement with all the policies.

The hammock crab net again netted no crabs. They'd been there, taken the salami and the smashed mussels, but none were entangled. Obviously I had to sit there dangling the net from the boat, and pull it up as I felt them crawling around. I needed a rigid crab trap, but all the ones I'd seen were too big to carry on the boat, so I'd have to design my own. Later I found two designs of folding crab traps, both made in Canada and for sale at the fine Ecomarine Ocean Kayak Centre on Granville Island in Vancouver, B.C.

My right arm was still numb at times. Hardening of an artery? How would you prevent that? I later learned to cut down on butter and eggs, cut the cholesterol. I had been a first aid instructor for years and felt confident I could handle most injuries, but this was something new. It wasn't until two months later that I read, in the first edition of *Sea Kayaking* by John Dowd, about "canoeist's arm," an advanced form of tendonitis. Prevention: Use unfeathered paddles, as it is only the arm that cocks the paddle that is affected. The condition's effects can be long-lasting. Later medical research showed many more causes of this ailment, but for the next two months I endured it and tried to both push and pull more with the left arm. I also trained myself to be ambidextrous, feathering the left blade and cocking my left wrist for an hour at a time as a relief for my right arm.

Now, years later, tendonitis has been researched extensively. For kayakers there are many ways to prevent it. Hold the paddle loosely, not in a death grip. Angle the feathered blades 80 degrees instead of 90. The wrist flexes vertically without problems; it's the sideways torque that does the damage, and a bent elbow can absorb some of that torque. Feather the blades only when paddling against the wind, unless you paddle

such a tippy boat that you frequently need to brace and always want to know that your paddle blade is in the same position.

It was pleasant when the tide changed and went my way at the same time I was making a natural late-morning departure to continue my journey. Of course that was a poor justification for being lazy, because the wind chop was up by noon, nullifying the tidal current.

I planned to stop at Bell Island Hot Springs resort and then to camp up in Bailey Bay in preparation for a cross-country hike to Lake Shelokum and the undeveloped wilderness hot springs reported to be near there. Five skiffs from the resort were out fishing and none of them bothered to come near. Tourists and newcomers to Alaska would assume I was just some man out paddling from his bigger boat or his cabin. Old-timers would recognize the incongruity of the solo inflatable kayak, would know that no one was living nearby, and would come over to check me out.

Paddling against a headwind was always frustrating: so much effort and such slow progress. No satisfaction lay in cursing the wind, or myself for starting late, or for doing this trip at all, so each time one of the sportfishing boats was near and ignoring me, I would chant in rhythm to my strokes, "Bloody bastards with engines. Bloody bastards with engines." Laughing at my own rage got me around to the resort, where the reception was unusually cool for Alaska. At least the water in the mossy cement pool was warm, though it smelled strongly of sulfur. Later a fisherman said that the management wanted wealthy yacht people, not drop-in small boats. As my yacht scarcely qualified, I paddled off. Since then the resort has become a private corporation, open only to members.

Four miles on I found a jewel of a campsite between two streams on the east side of Bailey Bay, a mile below the trailhead that led to Lake Shelokum. Chocolate lilies, scarlet Indian paintbrush, and yellow buttercups sprinkled color on the grass like decorettes on a cake; I leaped from rock to rock to avoid crushing them.

If no-see-ums were tiny, noiseless critters that were all mouth, then we had just met, and I smeared on bug repellent for the first time. After supper I built a small fire, then sat on a log watching the scene. A fish jumped, the stream chortled, a hummingbird dive-bombed my red shirt, an ember fell into the ashes. The sun sank below the ridge across the bay.

I woke at 2:00 am. It was too dark to read, but light enough to walk or paddle. I woke again at 4:00 with a constant cough. It was that touch with civilization at the resort. I brewed honeyed tea. At 5:30 the sun was touching the ridge.

By noon I was at Spring Creek, west of Lake Shelokum, sitting in the grass beside the three-sided shelter. Civilian Conservation Corps crews built it in the 1930s; a masterpiece of rough-log architecture, it had hand-split shake sides and roof, now silvery gray and brittle with age. Nearby, two hot springs boiled out of the ground. Stringy red algae trailed them down the steep slope, and sulfurous steam arose. The shallow, rock-dammed upper pool was too hot, and by the time the water reached the pool at the bottom it was frigid. There had been talk of building a series of small redwood or cedar tubs at staggered temperatures. On the topo map there are many higher lakes, and here at the shelter you could have a base camp for hiking cross-country above the thick forests of the shore.

All this was to the good, but the 2.5-mile trail to get to the place was the worst I ever hiked. An overgrown track, mud, rock slides, berry brambles, fallen trees, devil's club, log steps rotted and slippery with moss, and torrents to cross. The wide waterfall, sucking and swirling out of the lake, terrified me. That was the thunderous sound I'd heard in the morning that seemed to be on the east side of Bailey Bay, but was just the echo reverberating off the cliff there. In the muddy trail were fresh bear tracks. This was the Cleveland Peninsula, a part of the mainland, and I would have to return to the sea over the same trail. Take care, Aud. Even the critic carping on my shoulder is concerned.

Down at the trailhead I bucked a stiff wind and an incoming tide paddling back to camp and made a supper of a rich mussel chowder, then stayed alert for symptoms of "red tide" as I packed for the morning takeoff. Paralytic shellfish poisoning, PSP, would be a complicated way to do a simple thing like dying. The culprit is a dinoflagellate, *Gonyaulax catenella*, and a report from the University of Southern California's Sea Grant Program gave the specific evidence: "Shellfish living in a coastal area will ingest the dinoflagellates and store them in their viscera. Since shellfish don't use acid in their digestive processes, these tiny one-celled animals are not broken down to any significant extent."

Along comes man – hungry. He collects some of the shellfish for a fine dinner that evening. When these contaminated shellfish are eaten, the acid in the human stomach breaks them down, along with the dinoflagellates in their viscera. If only a few are eaten, the only effects are a passing nausea and stomach cramps. However, if a sufficient amount is consumed, death can occur within a few hours. The first signs are numbness or tingling of the lips, gums, tongue, and face, leading to respiratory paralysis and finally death. There is no known antidote or effective treatment other than artificial respiration.

The report continues for three pages. My own additional research confirmed that not all shellfish store the toxins, only the filter feeders – clams, mussels, oysters, and scallops. Shrimps, lobsters, and crabs are safe. There may or may not be a red color present in the water. There are no guarantees.

But several factors made me decide to eat mussels. They are tidal animals, out of the water for longer periods than the other filter feeders, and more cases of PSP occurred in the warmer and possibly more polluted waters of California and Oregon than up here. The symptoms usually occur within fifteen minutes of ingestion, unlike poisonous mushrooms, which have to get all the way into the small intestine before the symptoms appear – too late to upchuck. I was carrying syrup of ipecac to induce vomiting, to get them out of my stomach if the symptoms occurred. There was another reason. Delicious. I had eaten them every night in a small café in Brussels, Les Moules, where they were brought to the table in a steaming iron pot with a slab of butter, hot crusty bread, and a chilled glass of wine. The gourmet was ecstatic. I was willing to take the calculated risk. During the rest of the summer and frequently over the next 20 years I ate mussels with no ill effects. I never ate them within five miles of town – too many other chances of pollution. But as they say, no guarantees.

In the morning, Jerry Castle came by in his powerboat to check on my welfare and then gave me the 20-mile ride to Helm Bay, where I camped. The wind that day had been up to 30 knots. A mile up the bay from the boats that were taking refuge at the float was a flat campsite, and I sat there alone by a fire that night, scared. It was 10 miles from here to Caamano Point, and then eight across Clarence Strait.

"What if the wind and seas come up like today when I'm halfway across Clarence?"

And,

"Fear is more of a problem than the problem feared."

And,

"Sunshine will make a difference."

And,

"I can wait for good weather."

But I was afraid, a deep gut fear.

I slept well, wakened to rain, then packed and paddled the mile down to the Forest Service cabin and the float. The cabins were frequent now, here within easy reach of Ketchikan, but when I got to Baranof Island, there would be no cabins, and Baranof is noted for grizzly bears.

By the next morning, all of the boats moored at the floating dock had gone, leaving a quiet peace of no man-made sounds and a heightened awareness of bird songs, tree sighs, stream sibilance.

I left at noon, passed the old Rainy Day gold mine and a small bay with grass and warm sunshine. The wind was rising as I passed Smugglers Cove, feeling too pushed for time to check out the waterfall and trout pool I'd read about. Five more miles of headwind and I landed on the small island shown on the topo and the chart: They both showed a neck of water, but it would have to be at a very high tide.

Someone had made a clearing in the alder trees, sheltered from the wind. The remains of a cabin were there, but no water source, so they must have relied on rain catchment. A deer walked the beach and a mink skittered over the logs as I ate a simple supper and rigged for an early start. Tomorrow, Clarence Strait.

At 3:45 am I was up. No coffee or liquids. Not with a four- to five-hour paddle ahead and no place to pit stop. To pee at sea is difficult at best: It's never safe to take your hands off the paddle. At 4:45 I launched and in an hour was around my island and clear of Caamano Point. The pale full moon was setting over the snowy ranges far ahead. I'd not been aware of the moon these past weeks, so often was it clouded over.

The outline of Grindall Island was there, faintly closer than Prince of Wales Island behind it. Five miles to my left was the Guard Island Light, flaring every five seconds.

There were four wide straits to cross this summer: Clarence, Sumner, Chatham, and Icy. I'd made rules for nasty stretches of water where there were no easy landings, based on years of paddling rough seas, and I followed them now. Think: What was the weather like yesterday? It was OK, some wind. Go early before the wind picks up. I'm doing it. Paddle out for an hour, and if it looks bad, go back. Keep in mind the tide direction.

Out in the strait now; the water dark and deep below me. To the south is the infamous Dixon Entrance, a wide line of clear horizon, but through that passage often come storms from the whole Alaska Gulf, funneled and compressed between the islands to a greater intensity. On my right is the long expanse of Clarence Strait, 60 miles of bumpy water stretching away to the north.

I line up the Guard Island light against Vallenar Point, and move it back against the open water of Tongass Narrows as I paddle ahead. I've gone around Revillagigedo Island, finished the shakedown. Now is the test of that preparation and of all the years before. An hour out and still OK. By 7:00 am the wind has picked up a bit. What decision do I make if I'm halfway across and it gets nasty?

Go ahead, of course, unless it's a fierce headwind. I look back at Caamano Point. The wind and tidal current are setting me north. I shift the course to the south of Grindall, but keep moving ahead, paddling evenly, without a stop, without a pause. My watch dings the hour and I start counting strokes. An hour later, the count is 2,200, a pace of 37 strokes a minute. Keep it up.

I'm wearing the wet suit and booties, which give me a compressed body and cold feet. In the water they would be warmer than clothing, but once wet from a capsize, would they be warmer when I got back in the boat than the wool underwear and socks, covered with foul-weather gear and boots?

If I capsize, the essential thing is to get back in the boat. In this 48-degree water I might stay alive for an hour, but in far less time than that I'd go numb, lose consciousness, and be unable to climb back into the boat or do anything else to save myself. In the water it would be difficult to get the signal flares out of the emergency bag, and no one is near enough to signal to. Years later, I did get a small VHF radio so I could call for help.

In 20-knot winds in Hawai'i, I had practiced with and without a life jacket, righting the boat and sliding in over the gunwale after a deliberate capsize. It was far more difficult with the life jacket on; its bulk prevented an easy entry. Anything that stops me from getting back in the boat is not a life jacket. I have one with me. I'm not wearing it, but I am wearing a lifeline to make sure I stay with the boat. A dozen life jackets won't help me if I capsize and the wind blows this lightweight boat out of reach.

A 300-pound test line is looped over my left shoulder and under my right arm. The loop is spliced in, and the other end is spliced to a snap hook and clipped to the side of the boat. In case of a capsize, I'll lead the lifeline over the bottom of the boat, put one knee on the side, and pull on the line to flip the boat upright. Then I'll climb in, haul in the tethered paddle and supply bags, and go on. Great theory. I practiced it 10 times before this trip in the warm seas of Hawai'i. Not here. Three years later, on another trip, I do capsize and am back in the boat in 23 seconds.

I think my nine-foot Sevylor Tahiti Sport boat survived a short Alaska trip last year, has one patched seam that split and was mended, and seems fine so far. Only coming in through 8- to 10-foot breakers have I been dumped.

Still there might be that random wave... There are no "rogue" waves, according to Dixon Stroup, the Hawai'i oceanographer, only combinations of random waves. "Rogue" implies that it really isn't your fault, but anyone on the sea should expect a double-size wave occasionally.

A misjudged stroke on a crest? A too-friendly orca? What if a seam pops? That hasn't ever happened at sea; why should it now? Stop supposing. Stop thinking. Keep paddling. Each wave has to be judged and taken at the proper angle.

Twenty years later, rogue waves have been confirmed. They do happen.

I'm north of Grindall Island now and three-quarters across. The mind shifts to an old Hawaiian chant. *Hoe aku i ka wa'a*, "Paddle ahead the canoe." I wonder what the Haida Indians chanted in their cedar dugouts. I am north of Haida territory now, into Tlingit country. A mile to go and I turn south toward Grindall. Three hours now, 6,600 strokes without pause, every stroke with the full power of the back and shoulders.

Ahead, a boat comes out of Grindall Passage. She's the *Island Trader*, with a big rig on the stern like a derrick, a cargo boom perhaps. They yell something, but I can't catch it. I wave once and keep paddling – into the lee of the island, sheltered from the southeast wind. I slow the pace, watching the shore, find the charted buoy ahead and then the Forest Service cabin.

It is the poorest of all so far. Out of easy maintenance reach from Ketchikan, and often used as a refuge by fishermen, it gets frequent use. There is no ax, broom, sledge or wedge, and the wood supply is low. I suspect that some sport boater has some new tools. Cold and wet, I warm up with a fire and a change into dry clothes. I forage for wood along the steep shore in the forest and rebuild the woodpile, stirr the old ashes down and lay a new fire, and then launch again, to get more mileage in and cut off some of the 20-mile day tomorrow. I'm slowing down, easing the tension of the crossing.

Two hours later I had added six miles, aided by a tailwind. Finally I said, "That's it," and turned to shore, straight to a delightful site. It was a beach of rounded stones – no sharp barnacles or mussels, only the smooth pebbles shining in the clear water of the shallows, gleaming pink and gray in the evening light. From shore it had seemed to be a no-water camp, but at the edge of the forest there was an inch-wide waterfall into a clear pool, two feet across. It had no outlet, only seepage under the pebbles. I felt I should be an elf, poised there at the edge of my own lake.

By a level ledge for the tent was an alder to hang clothes on, an alder that would filter the morning sun into dappled shadows. Drift logs were there for a countertop and seat. I strung my hammock from springy limbs and lay watching the view across Kasaan Bay, then walked down to the water's edge and raised clasped hands in salute. The dreaded Clarence Strait was done. I had made it.

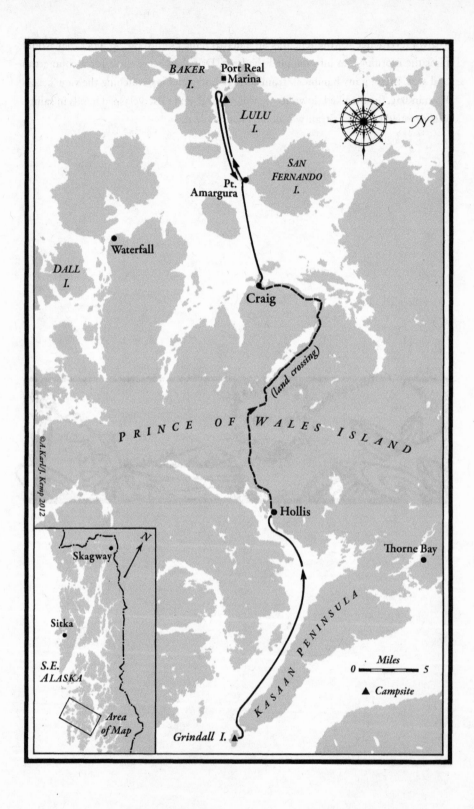

©A.Karl/J.Kemp 2012

Hot Springs Quest

All night long I heard the trickle of the waterfall. It was a small safe sound, not like the roar of the giant surf six months a year at home on the north shore of Oʻahu. Here the quiet was intense. Most planes flew so high that I heard no sound and could not see them, only their jet trails. Others passed, the little two- and four-seater floatplanes, the workhorse vehicles of southeastern Alaska, but their sound was low and distant. Fishing boats were frequent, but often too far away to hear.

This was Prince of Wales Island, third-largest island in the United States, surpassed only by Kodiak, farther north in Alaska, and by the Big Island of Hawaiʻi.

The paddle from my campsite to the ferry dock at Hollis was easy and in sheltered water; I caught a ride across the island to the small town of Craig, 30 miles on a paved road in the first car I'd seen in three weeks. Catching a ride was easy, with a rolled-up boat under one arm and four bags. At the post office, I picked up the letters from home and the resupply package that I'd sent from Hawaiʻi, then went out in a steady rain to buy eggs, lemons, onions, cheese, wine, and the few other fresh groceries and equipment I needed. In the meeting room of the Haida Way Inn, I sorted the piles, packed a box of gear, charts, and maps I no longer needed, and returned to the post office to mail them home.

A favorite author had lived in Craig. Ballard Hadman had sparked my interest in Alaska back in 1954, when I read her book As the *Sailor Loves the Sea*. Through the years I reread it, understanding it better as I learned more – about the sea, about fishing, about Alaska, and especially about the islands and waters of southeastern Alaska. The book was set in World War II; now Mr. Yates, who owned the Craig hardware store, told me about those times. Young Robbie Yates, a world traveler himself, was a volunteer at the local library, which he opened for me so I could see the old albums of the history of Craig. No pictures of the Hadman family, but another character, Shorty, was there, and some of the other people in the book.

I thanked Robbie and went through town to the Forest Service office, where they confirmed my next cabin stop and gave me an ax to replace the one they knew was missing. Their biologist, Tom Kogut, filled in information about plants and animals I'd seen. He'd been around most of this area in an open skiff, so had some understanding of what I was doing. It was a friendly office. Paddy Murphy and Cressy Wheeler gave more information and supportive comments. I liked Craig and wondered what spending a winter in a small Alaska town would be like. A lot would depend on the cabin, the people, and the library.

I packed the gear and lugged everything down through the rusty cables and trash on shore, then pumped up the boat and tied in the bags. I shoved one bottle of wine tightly into the bow and another into the stern. They fit perfectly into the triangle where inflated sides and hull came together, and were cushioned by the air-filled compartments. It was my wine cellar, my French cave, cooled by the icy water rushing by. With careful rationing I could make a bottle of wine last a week or more. That night's dinner was already planned, spaghetti Romano with a portion of red wine. Dinner tomorrow would be fondue with some of the white wine. Somewhere along with French classes in high school had come the concept of wine as food and part of a meal. It was also part of my epicurean spoof, and I sometimes wondered if it was the actual taste of wine I liked or if it was the long history of wine going back to the myths of Bacchus, or Dionysus, the poems of Omar Khayyâm, and the wine-and-candlelight idea of romance. There was also the visual and aural appeal, as the golden or claret-colored liquid glugged and swirled into the stemmed glass.

The seven miles to Point Amargura, on San Fernando Island, took three hours, in the best paddling conditions so far: a five-knot tailwind and easy ripple seas. Remember this, Aud, when you're swearing at headwinds in the next weeks. Once, you had it just right.

The cabin at Amargura was an A-frame with a loft. It probably got drop-in use by kids in boats, instead of hot-rod trucks, looking for a place to party. I swept it all and scrubbed the counter and table, mended the stovepipe and fitted it back together, then made a drift-log base to lift the stove so its pipe would reach the chimney outlet in the roof. I cleaned out the hardened accumulation of ashes and made a woodpile from driftwood, using my saw and the new ax.

Giant clumps of dark green fleshy staghorn seaweed had washed up on shore. In Hawai'i we call it wawae'iole, rat's foot. The scientific name is *Codium*, but what is the Tlingit name? I mixed it with fresh onion, soy sauce, pepper, and smoked salmon from Mrs. Yates's kitchen, and had it as a first course for dinner, before the spaghetti. No tomato sauce on this pasta, just olive oil and garlic, butter, pepper, minced parsley, and freshly grated Romano, all glistening and steaming.

The next morning the nearest freshwater was a half-hour paddle. On my way back to the cabin a whale went by a mile away. I landed at the cabin and brought up the boat. Ten minutes later the whale arrived, only 100 feet offshore. Did she feel the rhythm of the paddle and so come closer? She waved a fin. Humpback for sure. I waved back.

"Aloha, friend. Didn't I see you in Hawai'i last winter?"

On the east side of the small isthmus here at the southern end of San Fernando Island, I could look back to Craig, its clear-cuts vivid on the slopes above town. On the west side I sat with dinner and looked out toward my route tomorrow. West and southwest I could see Lulu, Baker, and Saint Ignace Islands. The brown contour lines on the flat paper topo map of Baker had leaped up into craggy peaks. The bays were deeply indented, nearly touching at their heads, a contorted coastline of cliffs and coves.

The fourth of my nine hot springs might be there, or maybe not. At least it was marked on the map of Baker Island, as Dalton Hot Spring. It was not listed in my Geological Survey thermal springs report, but it had been noted in the NOAA list of June 1980.

Why was this quest for hot springs so strong that I had built my route around them? Now that I was warm and dry and settled in, there was no urgency and the mind could drift. Perhaps it started with being born an Aquarius, then continued with having baths as a child in a galvanized washtub by the woodstove in the middle of the kitchen floor of our mountain cabin, but as I grew older, standard bathtubs were never very satisfactory. What good was a tub where you couldn't float, your knees got cold when you lay down, and you sat in your own dirty water?

Then in the 1960s I attended a job conference in Japan and was introduced to a home-style *furo*, a deep tub where you could float, weightless, with your knees effortlessly tucked under your chin and with hot water up to your ears. Since wood and other fuel to heat water were scarce, the Japanese had evolved a system of scrubbing themselves and rinsing clean before stepping into the tub, so that a family or community could soak one after another or together in the same hot tub. I had seen people on the street in Tokyo in December coming home from the public bath, clad only in a thin cotton kimono, steaming and beaming.

Later, back in Hawai'i, still gentled and tender from the courtesy of the Japanese people, I took a long weekend hike on the Big Island. There the workers on the Kohala irrigation ditch had built three shelter cabins along the 40-mile trail, and each had a simple wood-fired *furo*. The cabins no longer had live-in crews, but after I had hiked all day in the rain with a heavy pack, gathering wood was small payment for the sheer bliss of soaking in a deep tub, miles from the nearest other person.

At my own house I had rebuilt an old front deck and left one edge unfinished. It needed a *furo*, but the redwood hot tubs that had evolved from wine vats up on Mountain Drive in Santa Barbara were too expensive. A 55-gallon oil drum was too narrow. I could build a wooden tub, but outside by the sea, with frequent rain, it would always be slimy or salty.

Then one day I found it: an army mess hall aluminum cooking pot. It was lying on its side, full of dirt and leaves, in an abandoned pig farm. I asked around. No one claimed it. I went back a month later. OK. Long enough. I drove my VW van as close as possible, rolled the pot to it, lifted it in, and brought it home. It had a drain and legs, so I stood it on cement blocks, extended the deck out around it, then ran a hose from the laundry tub faucet to fill it until I could install proper plumbing. It is 27 inches in diameter and three feet deep, and filling it runs my gas water heater out of hot water. Someday I'll make a driftwood-fired heater for it.

But now I can sit on the redwood step, scrub, dip a wooden bucket to slosh and rinse with abandon, then ease into the tub, sliding down to a half sitting, half floating squat. It is impossible not to say, "*Mmmaaaahhhh.*" I look out at the moonlight on the sea, watch the reflection of palms in the water under my chin, and sip from a chilled glass of white wine. Sam, the cat, comes to lap water from the tub or tuck down companionably on the step.

A pool is eroded into a cliff on Moloka'i, but it is cool, not warm, and on the Big Island I floated one evening in a warm, pale blue pool near the sea, but too many people came and went along the trail. The history for my quest was set, but now I had a new dream of a forest pool, near the sea but miles from people, lined with smooth pebbles, steaming, waiting.

I stashed most of the supplies away from the cabin and packed for a three-day expedition, planning to return here after exploring Baker Island and before heading north. Out of the cove I had a headwind, blowing from the west and wrapping around both sides of Lulu Island. I stopped at Rana Reef, but saw none of the sea otters that Stephen Hilson notes in his great book, *Exploring Alaska and British Columbia.* Westerlies are supposed to die down early, but a westerly on the outside of Baker, open to the whole Pacific Ocean, could produce rough seas and crashing surf.

I was three weeks into the voyage now, but it felt like more. I made it halfway through Port Real Marina passage and quit for the day, thinking about all those Spanish names. In August of 1775, the explorer Bodega y Quadra, with a crew of 43, sailed into the area on board the 36-foot schooner *Sonora* and took possession for Spain. It was only one of many explorations in the area by Spanish, English, Russian, and American ships. Forty-three people on a 36-foot boat! I'm only one person on nine feet.

By that night the wind had eased. I was camped, well fed, and ready for bed. I'd made a fire and sat there wondering if the organic soil burned here as it did in Hawai'i. Later I found that it does indeed. A small gray vole worked toward me. I took a flash photo, wondering if birds, whales, mink, and mice would be the extent of my wildlife photos. Fine with me. Bears are too big and much too unpredictable. Humpback whales are gentle giants. Bears are not. It was only after 20 more years of paddling this country and 31 bears at closer than 100 yards that I came to a basic understanding of bears.

By 6:00 am I was at Pigeon Island, with rain and headwinds increasing as I paddled toward the northwest point of Baker Island. Swells were smashing on the rocks. I made a landing to check the surge, to see if I could land if need be on the outside of Baker. So far, it was still possible: wind 15 knots and choppy four-foot seas plus swells. It was four more miles to Outer Point, then three more to the ledge where I would land and go in search of Dalton Spring, or four if I paddled on into Veta Bay and walked back along the ledge.

In *As the Sailor Loves the Sea*, Ballard Hadman wrote:

> *"On we would troll off Baker Island. Next to Point Addington, Baker is my favorite. Towering contours, indented bays, lovely headlands: high, wild, uninhabited. At the base of gray stone cliffs at the head of one bay there is a mineral hot spring. It has a wooden tub sunk in it, a circumstance that intrigues me. A wooden tub sunk in a hot spring in surpassingly wild Baker Island in a bay fronting the whole western ocean. Who put it there? I should like to have a bath in it."*

I, too. Had she been writing of Dalton? It showed on the topo map as a quarter of a mile inland and not at the head of a bay. Is there another hot spring? Hadman's description was written in 1942, and her hot spring could have ceased bubbling by now, the wooden tub long since rotted away.

I was paddling directly into the wind, an uphill fight at a three-knot rate, but making less than one knot actual forward speed: six to eight more hours paddling, if it didn't get worse. Straight, southwest winds literally in my teeth, and rain, of course, driving into my face under the visor. Rain wasn't the problem. Wind and seas were the problem, and they were increasing. I was paddling up the side of Everest. I spent another hour of grunting effort, watching the shore for progress, lining up a tree against a mountain peak. It stayed there, unchanging.

I can't look at a painting of a seascape without evaluating it in terms of my kayak. Could I survive in that sea? Could I stay upright? Those foaming white crests and deep troughs delight the artist and terrify me. Would I choose to be out there? No! If I were caught out there? A hard paddle stroke might punch me through that toppling crest. The artist is elated, the paddler gut-wrenched.

I turned around, defeated, then gritted my teeth, turned back and fought it again for another half hour. Finally, defeated for good this time, I spun back again and headed for home, the cabin at Amargura. It wasn't until I was three-quarters home that I thought of the alternative, to get into that first little hook bay after the northern point of Baker and wait it out. It was not the first time I've failed to look for all the alternatives, been so daunted by the moment's events that I wasn't thinking in all directions. I had no heart to go back and try again.

I came back to the cabin and lit the fire I'd laid yesterday. Hot tea and rolls and change out of the wet clothes. It was so good to have the cabin and the old stove. I wondered about trying again. I needed to talk to fishing boats for information and weather forecasts, but they were usually out in midchannel while I was near shore. I put off the decision. I was still moving slowly. Lack of sleep wears me down more than hours of paddling. Maybe I could leave the hot spring project for my friend Mark Rognstad from Hawai'i, who was due to come this way in his own kayak. There were nine hot springs in my summer's route, I had found only two out of the first four.

Another super spaghetti was served that evening, this one with a sauce of reconstituted home-dried tomato sauce, oregano, wine, and diced Romano cheese. These slurpy homemade pasta dishes are very satisfying, and I've never yet found one of the prefab freeze-dried packs that is as good. I saved some of the sauce for a breakfast omelet, then mixed up a chocolate-chip cake from half a box of mix. There were two foil pie pans here, one for the lid and one for the bottom of an oven. I put the pan of cake batter inside and clipped the edges together. I shoveled coals up on top of the stove and set three rocks to hold the "oven" above them, then scooped more coals onto the oven lid, adding glowing ones as they faded.

In 20 minutes the cabin was filled with the aroma of warm chocolate cake. It worked! I wouldn't need to wait for a cabin with an oven to do baking. So far, out of six cabins, only one had had a cookstove with a real oven. Two others had old sheepherder-style stoves, two more the small, cylindrical Fire View brand, and the cabin at Helm Bay had a big Earth Stove – no oven there either.

Journal, Day 26: Made a fire and climbed back to bed in the loft hearing the comforting crackle. Hawai'i residents don't hear that sound, except those few with stoves and fireplaces up at the higher elevations, or those of us with a passion for an open fire even at sea level. The compressed logs supplied for the woodstoves in the National Park cabins in Haleakala on Maui neither crackle nor smell like real wood. You need to carry in a few cedar shakes or driftwood pieces from the beach, as the salt content of · driftwood helps the crackle factor.

I sat on the doorstep in the brief sun with coffee and a *New York Times* crossword puzzle. As the song said, there was nowhere else on earth that I would rather be. Yes, there were a few moments of contentment along with the grousing about wind and rain. I figured that a ratio of one good day to five hard ones was acceptable.

I wondered about paddling to Yeats's Lake Isle of Innisfree, in Ireland. Here, too, the water was lapping at the shore, and hummingbirds, not bees, were loud in the glade. In 1987, I would go to Ireland and paddle my new, 13-foot boat on Lake Gill and around tiny Innisfree. *Islet* is more accurate than *isle*. It's only about one acre in size and about two-tenths of a mile from Gill's south shore. A redheaded Irish boy, about 16, was rowing tourists around the isle in a big skiff. I loaned him my boat and he handled it as if he'd been kayaking for years. Church Isle or Cottage Isle, a mile away across the lake, were more of a size to have Yeats's "bee-loud glade," but Innisfree, meaning "Heather Isle," has more of an Irish lilt. I checked the latitudes. At Amargura, I'd been north of all of Ireland, at about the same latitude as Edinburgh, as Hamlet's castle in Denmark, as Moscow, and as Kamchatka in the northwest corner of the Pacific. In the southern hemisphere I'd have been below all of New Zealand and Australia, below the Falklands, on a latitude only with South Georgia and the southern tip of Chile, just above Cape Horn. I should be carrying an inflatable globe of the world.

Hmm, five places in the world with fjords: this British Columbia–Alaska coast, Norway, New Zealand, Greenland, and Chile. I'd hiked, not paddled, up Lyse Fjord in Norway. Only this coast and Chile's have an inside passage. In the others, you have to go out into a rough open sea to get from one fjord to another. Chile has hot springs, too.

What would the present day here in Alaska bring? Chocolate cake and Italian omelet for breakfast. Then the walk of 50 yards of mossy trail to the west cove: more surge on the shore today and water moving up from the south, with low dark clouds over Baker Island. An exploration of the peninsula's tip, where I found a crabapple tree among the tall spruce and hemlock, and patches of beach asparagus, *Salicornia*. Euell Gibbons called it glasswort in his *Stalking the Blue-Eyed Scallop*, the most useful food book for this whole coast.

Small trails through the woods were marked with abalone shells. With only 13 species of Haliotis in the world, it is an easy genus to learn. In California I had dived for three species, all larger than this small beauty, aptly named for its latitude, *kamchatkensis*. Did mink or otters pry them off the rocks and bring them back into the shelter of the woods to eat? Were there both sea and river otters here?

The wind still hadn't come up strong, but 10 to 15 knots here might be 20 to 25 outside Baker. I deflated and cleaned the boat, wiping out the slime of three weeks from the hidden bilge between sides and bottom, then repumped it. All was holding well. When a friend referred to it as a "rubber ducky," I'd bristled. Certainly the boat did look like a child's toy, but I had voyaged close to 1,000 miles in these Sevylor Tahitis, had paddled one in 15-foot seas and 30-knot winds, and I knew what they could do. They needed a lower profile in the wind and a foot-controlled rudder, but loaded evenly through their full length, they tracked adequately. They were a better whitewater river boat than a sea kayak. Sevylor soon stopped making this tough little Sport model and made other changes, which were not acceptable, but for now my $125 boat was doing fine. Of course you can get soggily sentimental about anything that gives you comfort or efficient performance every day. I've been known to hug a mug.

Dinner was a rehydrated Portuguese bean soup and lightly steamed beach asparagus with fresh hollandaise. I was eating 3,000 to 4,000 calories a day and losing weight. Two reasons: cold and work. Certainly I was burning more calories to keep warm here than I did at home. Sometimes I'd go swimming here, a fast naked crawl stroke out 10 yards and back, rather in the style and screaming speed of a hydrofoil. Does a dip a day keep hypothermia away?

As for work, I figured it out with pencil and paper the first week. If my cruising pace was 20 strokes per minute, and I was moving five pounds of water per stroke, then I was pressing 6,000 pounds of water per hour, and at the end of an eight-hour day would have moved 48,000 pounds, or 24 tons. Five pounds might be a low estimate, but my shoulders were hardening and my belly flattening.

In the afternoon I took some mail out to a boat that had been trolling back and forth in front of the cabin. I paddled almost into her path, just outside the trolling lines. A pretty blond girl in boots and watch cap was rinsing a bucket. I asked if they'd had any weather reports.

"Not for the past few days."

"Where are you headed tonight?"

"Craig."

"Could you tell me something about the west side of Baker Island?"

"Haven't been out there."

There was no smile, no friendliness, no slowing down. The man at the wheel was grim-faced. I didn't ask them to mail the letters I had on my lap in a plastic sack, but wished them well and paddled away. I suspected that fishing had been poor, that they thought I was some rich dilettante paddler off a yacht, and that I had no comprehension of their hard work. I could understand how they felt. I fished commercially back when the sardines and the tuna disappeared from California waters, and I know what a hard, nasty, and sleepless – but satisfying – life it can be. We averaged $40 a month fishing income over three years. But I'd worked many more years to save enough money to get here now, in my own boat, alone, and in my own style.

Back on the beach, and only 10 minutes later Mark Rognstad came ashore in his inflatable Semperit Dolphin, and 10 minutes after that, two men came in from the west cove, where they'd beached their open skiff. They fished and trapped out past Noyes Island, out in the elements with no warm cabin on their boat or on shore. They were friendly and knowledgeable and moved with the quiet assurance of men who live close to the earth. They said they were getting lottery land in Edna Bay to the north.

This was a sudden shift from solitude, but the two fishermen left, and over dinner Mark gave me an account of his voyage from Ketchikan, including a long portage from Twelvemile Arm to Trocadero Bay, and then the paddle here to Amargura as we'd scheduled back in Hawai'i. As we talked, Mark's engineering training kept him sifting through mutual problems of boat and gear to ingenious solutions. He planned to search for the hot spring the next day while I went north toward Sea Otter Sound. By six o'clock the next morning he was paddling out of the west cove. With a sleeker, tougher boat and far more muscle power, he made an average three knots to my two, and was out of sight in half an hour.

Alone again.

Spaghetti Romano

½ lb spaghetti or linguine or other pasta
10 cloves minced or mashed garlic
3 tablespoon olive oil
3 teaspoon minced parsley
1 cube (¼ lb) butter. (Get the best butter, preferably Anchor butter from New Zealand)
Pepper (Carry your own small pepper grinder)
Grated Romano cheese

Cook pasta in salted water, or use ½ seawater, until as done as you like it. Drain. While cooking, simmer garlic in olive oil. Do not brown. Sprinkle parsley onto drained pasta. Melt butter on top of pasta. Pour on the garlic and olive oil. Mix. Season with pepper and top with Romano. Serve with a good red wine, preferably a shiraz.

Portuguese Bean Soup

1 quart water
1 8-oz. can tomato souce
1 large onion, cubed
2 potatoes, cubed
1 carrot, cubed
1 ½ teaspoons salt
½ teaspoon pepper
1 teaspoon paprika
2 15-oz. cans kidney beans
1 hot Portuguese sausage, approx. 12 oz, sliced

Prepare at home: Combine all ingredients except sausage in a pot, bring to a boil and cook until tender. Put half of soup into blender and purée. Return to pot. Dry finished soup in a food dryer until dry and crumbly. Dry slices of hot Portuguese sausage and pack separately, or take along a fresh sausage, or a 5-oz. can of ham.

In camp: Add soup mix to 3 cups water. Add ham or dried sausage. Bring to a boil and simmer 5 minutes. If using fresh sausage, slice and add after simmering.

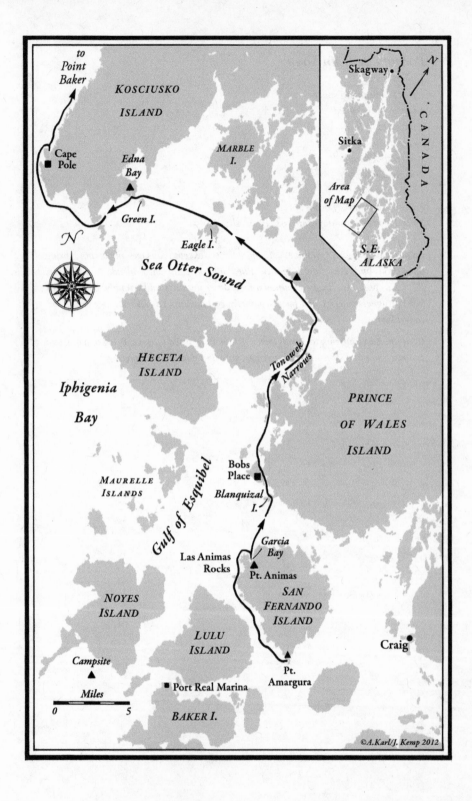

to
Point
Baker

KOSCIUSKO
ISLAND

Cape
Pole

Edna
Bay

MARBLE
I.

Green I.

Eagle I.

Sea Otter Sound

HECETA
ISLAND

Iphigenia
Bay

Tonowek
Narrows

PRINCE
OF WALES
ISLAND

MAURELLE
ISLANDS

Bobs
Place

Blanquizal
I.

Gulf of Esquibel

Garcia
Bay

Las Animas
Rocks

Pt. Animas

NOYES
ISLAND

SAN
FERNANDO
ISLAND

Craig

LULU
ISLAND

Campsite

Miles

0   5

Port Real Marina

Pt.
Amargura

BAKER I.

©A.Karl/J. Kemp 2012

Skagway

Sitka

CANADA

Area
of Map

S.E.
ALASKA

SEA OTTER SOUND AND SHIPLEY BAY

It was time to head north. Like Stuart Little, the mouse in E. B. White's children's story, I felt that north was the right direction. Soon I was away, heading up the west side of San Fernando Island, paddling quietly in warm sun through shallow water. Too shallow! I scraped on a razor-sharp barnacle, and after an hour I realized I was sitting lower in the boat. I pulled ashore, deflated the hull, patched the half-inch slice, pumped it up again, and was back in the water within an hour. A year later, the patch was still holding perfectly.

"Barnacles are not what they seem," says Maitland Edey in Time-Life's *The Northeast Coast*. "Since they sit in one place inside a shell, one might assume that they are something like clams, mussels, and snails – that group of hard-shelled, soft-bodied sea creatures called mollusks. But barnacles are not mollusks. They are arthropods, as different from clams as they are from camels. Indeed they are more closely related to a mosquito than to a mussel." I hadn't figured out yet how to eat a barnacle, so I was mostly concerned with avoiding their sharp shells.

By three o'clock, clouds covered the sky and a northwest wind was picking up. I fought my way around Point Animas, then continued two more miles. The Las Animas rocks were a place to return to. For the first time, I wished for my old gear of so many expeditions in Hawai'i: fins, mask, and snorkel. Here were small coves of yard-deep water with a sandy bottom, where the sun's warmth could heat the sea to 55 degrees, according to my thermometer. Tropical! Carmine sea urchins shone brilliantly against the sea's green, identifiable by a name as formidable as their spines, *Strongylocentrotus franciscanus*. Intricate animals, another example of the endless variety of earth's creations.

Across the wide Gulf of Esquibel the wind blew toward me, whipping the seas into a frothy chop. In Garcia Bay I landed three times before I found a campsite – deep in the bay, but complete with blueberries that promptly went into dumplings.

Always I realized that this was a known wilderness that had been paddled and tramped and motored by Tlingit, by miners, and by fishermen, at least along the coast. But it was new country to me, and that was what mattered now. At my pace I saw a town only once every two or three weeks, so the wild isolation of the islands and the forest was far more evident to me than to people in a fast power boat who could go from the town of Craig to the settlement of Point Baker, at the north end of Prince of Wales Island, in a day.

I woke to wind at two in the morning, at four, and at six. Each time I decided I might as well go back to sleep. At seven I looked out again and muttered, "If it gets better, I'll go."

Then, shrugging, "If it stays the same, I'll go, but not until after a good breakfast."

It stayed the same, and the three-mile crossing of the edge of the gulf was as smeared with chop and whitecaps as the night before, but my belly was full, and I'd tucked flowers into each of the bow lacings to fortify my morale. The gulf seemed enormous, seven miles out to the western islands and seven miles north to Heceta Island, with not even a fishing boat in sight. It didn't really matter. I had told my kayak classes, "You can drown in two minutes, so it doesn't matter if people are five minutes away, or 50 miles. You've got to be able to save yourself."

In the lee of the Blanquizal Islands, I watched a salmon that seemed to be rounding up a school of herring. A mile away a whale blew, moved west, and then circled and came back behind me: a humpback with white on the dorsal area. This for once was a familiar animal. About 2,000 of them do what I was doing, winter in Hawai'i and migrate north to summer in Alaska. They don't really have a humped back, but they do make steep dives from the surface that make the dorsal fin appear to be humped over. Unlike orcas, porpoises, and sperm whales, they have no teeth, and instead strain food from the water with a flexible fringe in their mouths called baleen, the "whalebone" used in 19th-century corsets. In Alaska they feed; in Hawai'i they breed and give birth to their young, though so far no scientist has witnessed a mating.

The orca that came within five feet of my boat, and boot, in Behm Canal could have been 30 feet long. This humpback might be as long as 45 feet and might weigh 40 tons. When she was 200 feet from me, she turned and went out beyond the Blanquizals. I was hoping for a closer look and whistled and sang odd minor-key melodies, trying to imitate the whale songs I'd heard on records. I also sang "Aloha 'Oe." She rose suddenly 50 feet in front of me, blew, arched, and dove toward me, her huge flukes dripping, as I took photos. My singing quavered a bit, for her head must have been right under my boat, but she stayed underwater, having satisfied her curiosity. She had obviously come in to inspect, but I was not edible to a baleen whale, and so she went on.

On to Bobs Place, as marked on the topo map. Often on this voyage I wished I could have been here back in the 1920s, when more people were out in the isolated spots, fishing from skiffs, raising foxes on the small islands, panning for gold – people by themselves, or in pairs or families, living close to the land, before TV or helicopters or floatplanes. Today, only a few logs and boards remained as mementos of their presence.

"Who was Bob?" I asked aloud. "You must have felt, as I do, the presence of the small islands and the sheltered passages, the rise and fall of the tide, and the hum of bees feeding on thimbleberry blossoms. This is not a gold-mining place. You must have used rain catchment for water. How long were you here and why did you leave? Was it a good place for drop-in company, this corner of an island, on the route from Craig up to Sea Otter Sound? Were you Tlingit? Where are the records of the people who lived in these remote places, or are they only in the memories of people now old and dying?"

I was paddling north now, feeling again that north was right after the west of the past week. A small powerboat planed toward me and settled lower as it slowed. Brian, Sue, and Greg from the Little Naukati Bay lumber camp were going to Craig, so I gave them letters to mail. Questions and answers, then they sped south and I slogged north.

The tide was swirling into Tonowek Narrows, with whirlpools forming, deepening, overlapping, and disappearing. On an islet to my left a mossy, leaning post marked the grave of Chief Tonowek. Some Alaskans say that if you throw coins or snuff into the water his spirit will let you through the narrows. If you are too stingy, his tiderips will suck you under or spit you back out. It sounded like some of the instant legends of Hawai'i, but I dutifully tossed some coins I'd packed in my bib pocket that morning, and slipped by.

Paddling around the bay at Indian Gardens, I found bogs, not campsites. Farther on was Karheen Cove, the site of an old village, but it was overgrown and wet. Ahead was an islet just offshore with a gravel spit facing me, a level place to camp. Tired and discouraged, I would have tried to hitchhike if any boat had come by, but after hot soup and a thorough study of Sea Otter Sound on the chart, it all looked more possible. At sunset, using the self-timer of my sturdy little Fujica HD camera, I took a self-portrait, a pensive silhouette against the orange sky, not sure why I was taking all the pictures. So I could share this place with others? Maybe it was just for my own slide show, to go with the journals, at age 90.

In the morning the chill air was from the east. Just what I needed, a tailwind. I calculated a route across the sound that included islands for refuge in case of heavy weather. The sky was getting heavier by the minute, the overcast settling into a thick fog with a scant 100 yards of visibility. I figured the slight drift of the tide, and from the chart made a corrected compass bearing for Eagle Island to the west. It was simple navigation that had worked a dozen times, although I still doubted that I really knew what I was doing. Later I picked up a brochure from Silva Compass Company and decided to teach myself the correct system. Lo, it was what I'd been doing all along.

So now I placed the compass on top of the blue bag between my knees and headed out. In an hour Eagle Island appeared out of the mist, right on course, its contours matching those on the topo map. A small boat appeared and slowed to see if I was OK. Rosie, Jerry, and Roger were food-fishing for the day. Two 50-pound halibut, a red snapper, and a black cod were evidence of their skill. They filleted the cod and gave it to me with good wishes, revved up their engine to full power, and zoomed off. I revved up to full paddle power and made a pit stop on the island at a timber-loading beach – a mess of logs, mud, and discarded cables left by the last clear-cutting crew – then took a bearing on Green Island, five miles ahead.

In two hours the island's shape softly emerged from the mist, but there were no campsites. I rechecked the chart. I could veer off three miles to Edna Bay in the hope of finding people or shelter, but a cove was closer. My foul-weather gear was either condensing or sieving through to a wet, cold body. Reason and instinct both said "cove," and it was a jewel, tucked back into a quiet inlet.

I flung the tarp over a small, leaning spruce so that my ceiling was a silver mosaic of needles under a green skylight. Thrown up by storms, an old cable spool served for a table, a stump for a stool, and a 2-by-12-foot plank for a kitchen counter. The cod fried up delicately sweet and crisp, the rice filled me up, and the Kosciusko Island water was clean and sweet.

A red headed merganser herded her brood along the clear inlet, green in its deep center and gold-reflecting at the edge from the rockweed on the low-tide shore. I walked up to the stream to fill the water bag and found bear scat, but I was learning to accept it as standard. A hot pot shower and off to bed in the tent, staked out 30 yards away from the cooking area.

I planned for Cape Pole or Point Hardscrabble tomorrow, out from sheltered water, out on the edge of Sumner Strait. I had run off my charts and maps, except for a small-scale one, as I had originally planned to go through El Capitan Pass, but at Craig I'd been able to make a last-minute reservation for the cabin at Shipley Bay. When I got there I was going to repack and make a big bundle to send home, and I was going to get dry.

Outside the calm inlet the wind was up again. I had forgotten the facts of life. Through Straw Pass and out into the real ocean, no more sounds or bays. Here was a maze of islands with white surf breaking, sloshing over the flippers of seals on the rocks, surging through the narrow passes. A fishing boat was heading out into Sumner Strait. To the west was the immense bulk and beauty of Warren Island, looking wild and untouched. Ahead was a cove with a sand and rock beach, a good landing – and treasures. A crisp apple was washed up by the tide, then a big cod, gaffed but with the heart still beating. It must have dropped from the boat. No sense wasting good meat, so I filleted it out on a flat rock. Opportunism takes odd forms. Once on the Big Island of Hawai'i I found four wild piglets, freshly DOR (dead on road), so I had pork for dinner. In the San Juan Islands near Seattle, rabbits have proliferated, but road kill stew keeps the highways clean.

This southwest corner of Kosciusko Island was near the edge of the whole Gulf of Alaska. Except for the end of Warren Island and the curve of the earth, I would be able to see all the way home, across 2,000 miles of open ocean. Thinking of home brought images of flowers. There, it was fragrant plumeria and ginger; here, it was shooting stars, columbine, and a chocolate lily, a kind of fritillaria.

Out of the cove. Still rough. Now I knew why boats heading north take the inside El Capitan Pass instead of coming out here. I paddled through kelp and around the rocks with a lumpy sea and a crosswind of 15 knots. At sundown I turned into the lumber camp bay of Cape Pole, which had many buildings but few people. I heard later that it was a slack period, with most of the population gone. I hesitated to approach strangers and paddled on. It was time to camp and the tide was high. Good: Not so far to carry gear.

On a small island I was about to unload but – *unh*! a black bear squatted 100 feet away across the channel.

"Hul-lo."

And.

"You're supposed to run away."

And then.

"Go away!"

She looked at me and kept on munching greens. I turned on the camera flash, paddled closer, and took a photo. Madame Bear was a ham. She posed nicely and went on chewing. I decided to camp elsewhere: I had fresh fish in my pack and at low tide my islet would be part of the main island, with a clear walkway between. Bears here were probably accustomed to the people and the garbage dump of Cape Pole. Less wary, they were more dangerous.

Brown bears, grizzlies, are usually bigger, stronger, and more irascible than black ones. In an iffy situation you want to know which is which. Tell by the color? No, brown bears sometimes have very dark pelts, and black ones are often brownish. The difference is obvious in the humped shoulder of the brown and its dished face, compared to the straight nose of the black. According to Alaskans, one way to tell the difference is to climb a tree to get away: The black bear will climb up after you; the brown bear will push the tree over. So the story goes.

After two more miles I bivouacked for four hours' sleep. Carrying down the first load in the morning, I came around a seaweed-covered rock and startled a mink at eye level, three feet away. Fifty times larger, I could enjoy the small, lithe animal more than she could appreciate this huge fuzzy creature looming so close.

Through the kelp and around the points, I figured three hours to Ruins Point and three more to the head of Shipley Bay. Certainly the lack of sleep would slow me down as much as the wind on the port bow. Past Ruins Point I made a hard right, and the wind was then astern.

I raised the nylon kite sail and napped one minute at a time with a west wind pushing us. The kite was a charming toy, but paddling with this rare tailwind was faster. I couldn't paddle and sail at the same time, as the kite needed one hand to hold it. I would need a cleat and a quick-release knot. Sailing was a fine idea, in theory. Certainly Alaska had enough wind, but real sailing, upwind or crosswind, required leeboards or a keel and a rudder. In this light and tender boat it also added to the possibility of capsize. As a day sport in warmer waters, it would be good fun.

At home in Hawai'i I had once rigged a bamboo mast, a lateen sail, a paddle blade for a leeboard, a half-paddle rudder, and had spent a hilarious day with David Lewis. We capsized as often as we progressed and were laughing so hard we fell overboard at the possibility that someone might see Lewis, the internationally famous transatlantic, round-the-world, and Antarctic single-handed sailor, author of *Ice Bird* and *We the Navigators*, in this ridiculous rig. People laughing at themselves are very endearing, and David did it with gusto. Later, when David consulted with the crew of the first

Tahiti voyage of the replica voyaging canoe *Hokulea*, he came to my old beach house to tell me the details.

I searched the land ahead to figure out from the contours where the cabin might be. It was likely near a water supply, and a high valley ahead might be where Shipley Lake drained into a stream. From two miles away I saw an orange shape on the beach. At one mile I could see people. I landed, suddenly very conscious of being dirty, salty, and shapeless in the presence of seven very masculine, civilized men. Their fishing vacation was over; they'd be leaving by plane in the morning.

Despite their stories of bear sightings, I camped by the north stream, washed body and hair, strung a line to dry clothes, then walked over to the cabin to share a supper of their fish, my fish, and their wine. For dessert it was my dried papaya and pineapple, soaked, simmered in honey and butter, and then flamed with rum.

These men, all old friends who picked a place each year to adventure together, were doctors, teachers, and executives, and their conversation was as enjoyable as the supper. When their plane came in the morning, I waved good-bye and moved into the cabin. A day to stay out of the weather, slather with lotion, launder, putz, mend, and cook: a day to not paddle.

Cabins should have the sea in front and a stream in back and a window view of each. On the deck should be a place to sit with arms hugging knees while watching the changing light. This cabin fit all the criteria – a 10-point place. Across the bay was the granite spire of Mt. Francis, an angular sculpture nearly 3,000 feet high. Streams flowed on each side of the cabin, one with cutthroat trout, the other with a clam flat at its mouth. Between them was a curving green path out to a grassy knoll over the water – another place to watch the sea, the mountain, or the sunset. It was also a place to curl up with someone warm and tender. Sigh. The best part of a man's anatomy is that curve just forward of his shoulder where my head fits. After so many years of solo slogging, I sometimes fantasized about being taken care of. I have that curve, too, where a child's head fits, and often has.

Inside were bunks for six and a small woodstove with an oven. The men had complained that the stove didn't get hot, but after I cleaned the soot out from under the oven, found all three damper systems, and used hard alder wood instead of spruce, it got glowing red. I needed the warmth if I was going to sit and catch up on the journal. I am not Zhivago.

Lunch was that standby of all solo cooks, baked potatoes – no preparation, no utensils, no garbage. The lore of woodstoves came back. Top left of the oven is 450 degrees, top right 400, bottom right 350, bottom left 300.

No sun now: cloudy overcast and a wind. As I walked back from the stream with two jugs of water, the paddler said aloud, "I'm very happy."

And the cynic replied, "Remember that when you're paddling against the wind."

Journal, Day 33: A continental breakfast of the last roll with coffee. I hope that as I get rested and see the lake and the petroglyphs that Pat and Larry spoke of yesterday, and dig clams, and get all the gear sorted and dried, the desire to push on will come back. Just now I'm very content to be in here with the cold rain out there. Rain often means less wind though, and I'd rather have rain than wind.

In the afternoon I went to the lookout to see the changing, misty light on Mt. Francis. Below the knoll I got my second sight of a red headed merganser, paddling with her babies curving out in a fluffy train behind her. She quacked suddenly and sharply. They all scurried to her and dove, as an eagle wing-braked with his talons down, a foot away from her fierce upflung beak. The eagle flew off, defeated.

The stove continued to intrigue me. How should the chimney pipe be put together? Should the crimped edge that fitted into the next section be at the top or the bottom? Ole Wik's book on woodstoves says to put the crimped edge aiming down, because the soot and moisture running down and catching around the outside of an upward crimp rusts the pipes out.

On the table was a delicate little skull, complete with jawbone and precision-fit teeth and all of the cranial bones. I studied it and wonder who left it here. Mink, I think.

Panic. A boat was coming. Three loggers from Cape Pole were checking to see if the sockeye salmon were running yet. Mike was an articulate blond mechanic, Randy operated the huge machine that lifted the logs onto the trucks, and Bob was a newcomer trying to learn his role. A good conversation, then they left. Why my panic? It wasn't a human's social fear, but that of an animal whose lair has been discovered and solitude disturbed, evaluating and adjusting to new unknowns.

In the evening light I walked along the shore to the petroglyphs, the rock carvings made by unknown natives years ago on a rock near shore, a half mile west of the cabin. What a country this is! A sense of people here for centuries before me, yet all of them had fitted in, belonged, using this world in such small ways that it remained as if untouched until this century, with its long-lasting effects from logging and commercial fishing. Could the earth still heal itself? In a hundred years, if we ceased gouging ever deeper, would the clear-cuts grow tall and the waters again come alive with fish? I made a rubbing of one of the old designs, using a stuff sack for canvas and crushed ferns for coloring. No sign was left on the rock of my presence.

It was partly sunny, with light winds from the west. The mind and body absorb these things. There was no thinking process like "The wind is blowing the trees. They are bending toward the east. It is a west wind." Instead, it all osmosed into the subconscious, and the body walked on, skin moist from the air and hair ruffling like an animal's fur in the wind.

There was always a heightened awareness when I was alone, but it was even more intense when the sun was shining – as if the added distance I could see in miles outward also went inward behind the eyes and clarified the mind as well.

Fruit Dumplings

1 cup yellow cake mix, Bisquick, Krusteaz pancake mix or homemade mix
1 cup dried fruit. (apples, cherries, apricots, etc.)
2 cups fresh fruit (blueberries, salmon berries, huckleberries, apples or mixed fruit)
¼ cup sugar
2 teaspoons cornstarch

Simmer fruit in two cups water until tender. Stir together sugar, cornstarch and two tablespoons water, and add to fruit. Add ⅓ cup water to the cake mix. Drop batter by spoonfuls into simmering fruit. Cover tightly and cook for 15 minutes. Serve warm.

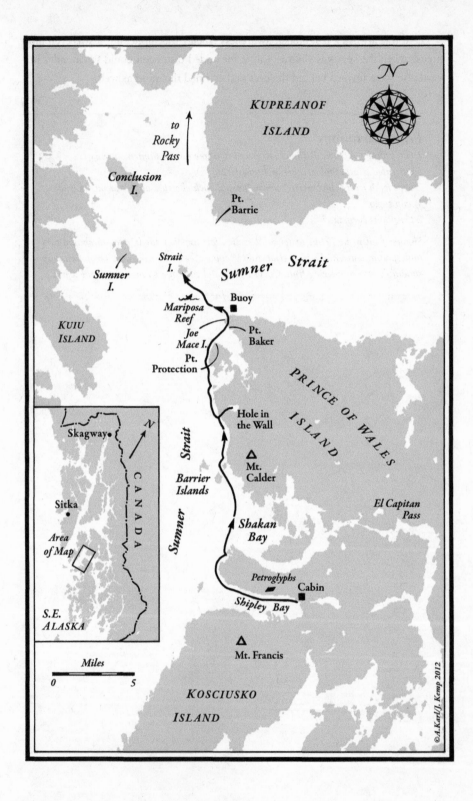

N

KUPREANOF
ISLAND

to
Rocky
Pass

Conclusion
I.

Pt.
Barrie

Strait
I.

Sumner   Strait

Sumner
I.

Buoy

Mariposa
Reef

KUIU
ISLAND

Joe
Mace I.

Pt.
Baker

Pt.
Protection

PRINCE OF WALES

Hole in
the Wall

ISLAND

Mt.
Calder

Skagway

N

Sumner   Strait

Barrier
Islands

El Capitan
Pass

C A N A D A

Sitka

Shakan
Bay

Area
of Map

Sumner

Petroglyphs   Cabin

S.E.
ALASKA

Shipley   Bay

Mt. Francis

Miles

0   5

KOSCIUSKO

ISLAND

©A.Karl/J.Kemp 2012

SUMNER STRAIT TERROR

It was time to get on with the journey, but there was one last place to explore here in Shipley Bay. I walked up the boggy trail to the lake. Fallen trees blocked its lower end, and the trail stopped in thick underbrush. An old aluminum skiff was there, but it was missing one oarlock. Coming back, I considered fishing for trout from the log bridge near the cabin, but I had plenty of food and hadn't been hooked into sportfishing.

I left at noon, planning on six hours' paddling to a camp at Indian Village peninsula, figuring that if the weather got worse, I could camp at the point before Shakan Bay. I didn't have to wait long for the weather. The wind shifted to the east and picked up until I was working hard to steer in a 30-knot half gale – with gusts to 40. I couldn't go back against that wind. I could have come ashore, but the boat was handling the seas well. In this small bay, the waves had no fetch to build up into mountains. To give the boat stability and to lower the center of gravity, I slid down as flat as I could, and to keep the wind from tearing the paddle out of my hands, I reversed my grip, with my fingers curled up forward.

Finally, I came ashore at the northwest corner of Shipley Bay. No way was I going out into Sumner Strait in that wind. I carried up all the bags of gear, then the boat on my windward hip, with the lifeline looped over one shoulder. I could scarcely stagger along with the wind bending the nine-foot boat halfway around me. Without the line, had I lost hold, the boat would have gone flying and bouncing away. Up among the trees I waited, munching dried fruit. The wind didn't ease, but around the point there should be a little lee. I hauled it all back down, launched again, and, hugging the shore, paddled on to a cove just short of Shakan Bay. At the head of the cove, by a stream, I checked sites, but all had piles from recent bears. Back at a sandy beach, I set up only the tent. It was midnight and I slept poorly, alert to every snapping twig, with thoughts of bears and wind.

Up and under way at six o'clock with no breakfast, just water. I was through the islands and out into Shakan Bay with a 15-knot wind from the east. Three miles across – an hour and a half – and I was into the rocks and islets below the Barrier Islands; then I slid through a channel on the seaweed and on around to the beach. Mt. Calder, another granite spire, 3,000 feet high, was directly above. I gathered mussels and steamed them, then napped for 20 minutes.

These en route naps are never simple. If the tide is coming in I have to tie an extra-long line to the bow, and then tie the other end to a rock, well up the beach. If I misjudge, then in 20 minutes I may have to wade out over my boot tops to undo that rock anchor point. If the tide is going out, I tie the line end to a rock and drop the rock in three feet of water, then paddle in, hoping that the length of the line will get me into water shallow enough for the height of the boots and hoping that I'll wake up before the boat is stranded dry, which would necessitate unloading everything to refloat the boat again, then reloading. I'd trained my mental alarm to ding every 10 minutes to check on all systems. As often as not, I miscalculated and paid for it in time and effort, and wet socks.

The wind calmed, and I paddled in good conditions to Hole in the Wall and through its slot. The narrow, high-sided pass opened out into a grass-lined bay. It would be a good place to anchor for a bigger boat, but I had learned that grass flats often meant mud, not campsites, so I paddled on out and north. I met a family in a skiff with an outboard, coming from the logging camp at Labouchere Bay to check on their crab pots in Hole in the Wall. They detoured over to see if I was OK. Law: The smaller the boat, the more concern for other small boats. A man with his wife and kids in the boat is in a caring frame of mind, and will come to check out a lone paddler. Men by themselves don't seem to care about another loner, and seeing my bulky cap from a distance, they never knew I was female.

Among the islands before Labouchere Bay I squeaked through a passage, sliding over the thick fronds and stems of bull kelp. Kelp was not a problem; I liked its sturdiness. I didn't know that it would later save my life.

On the eastern, calm side of a small island was a white gravel beach with flowers scattered up in the grassy woods, a place for a picnic and beer-can evidence that someone else thought the same. A path led back through to the strait and the blue expanse. To the northwest was a soft white peak, 4,000-foot Mt. Ada on Baranof Island, 50 miles away across the nearby azure of Sumner Strait, across the lighter gray-blue of the Kuiu Island range, and beyond Chatham Strait. In a week I would be there.

I picked up the cans, came back to the boat, and paddled off, pausing to fill and sink the cans in deep water. A seaplane came in with a roar, low over my head, and landed at Labouchere logging camp. Even though I had seen the buildings of the camp, it was still a shock when I came around the next point and saw a clear-cut slope, like a lovely woman whose head is shorn. It was not until years later that I flew over the interior of Prince of Wales Island and saw its devastation of logging roads and clear cuts. Most of the wood goes to Japan, to be made into chip or pulp board.

I live in a wooden house. I'm willing to give up redwood and its quality of being more resistant to termite attack – but I do need some wood. We have a similar problem in Hawai'i. So much of the native ohia and koa has been cut. Now we plant eucalyptus in tree farms, which will be good only for pulp, not for beautifully grained lumber for building furniture and Hawaiian canoes.

In another hour I was around White Bluff, getting tired and fighting an outgoing tide. I was lightweight now, on the last day before I picked up my second resupply box, at Point Baker. I slipped into a corner of Point Protection, named by Vancouver when he and his ship found refuge there from a storm in September of 1793. I climbed out on a rock to rest the buttocks, then headed across the bay to Joe Mace Island and found a campsite. I hauled up the gear, leaving it invisible from the sea, and then, carrying only money, went on to check on the next day's post office hours.

The town of Point Baker, named by Vancouver for the second lieutenant of the *Discovery*, consisted of a few buildings on floats. They housed a store, a café-bar, a laundry and shower, a fuel dock, and a post office that was officially third-class but had a top-notch postmistress.

Gayle's hamburger in the café was also first-class. Not the usual soggy prefab of a McJack King in layers of packaging thicker than the burger, but a flavorful bun, of substance, not air; a slab of juicy rare meat; and layers of crisp lettuce, onion, and tomato. It seemed longer than two weeks since I'd had my last fresh meal.

Out on the dock, the townsfolk were having a barbecue. There was Bill from down the channel (the gut), Mary O., with her own single-hander boat, George Nelson, Edra, Jeanette and Bill Dobson, Ruth Love, and the bearded Flea. I visited awhile, then paddled back to camp.

The post office would only be open from noon to three tomorrow, and the high tide in this area would be 10.5 feet at 3:59 pm. With any wind from the east, I'd need an incoming tide from the west and then the high slack period to make it across the five miles of Sumner Strait to Point Barrie. If I got my resupply box at noon, sorted and packed, and left by one, I should be OK. Here in this sheltered quiet water, with only a gentle rising and lowering of the tidal water, it all seemed easy. Strait Island was out there in the middle of Sumner Strait – west of my planned course, but it might be an emergency stop.

A deep sleep that night. Small islands like this, close to people, didn't require wariness about bears. At 10:00 am I loaded and paddled off for the post office, stopping at Bill and Ruth Love's place, with its well-kept compound of a garden, the fishing boat *Whidby*, and a warm house where a dozen projects were under way. When I asked Ruth about her fertile garden soil in this rocky area, she laughed, "Bill brings a sackful home on the boat whenever he gets some place he can dig it. Then I mix it with seaweed, compost, and the small amount of soil here, and it comes out fine."

Promptly at twelve o'clock I picked up the resupply box, then tied up at the Loves' dock to sort and repack. Fastened to a floating dock, talking to people, I was not as conscious of time as I was when alone on a shore where the tides floated or stranded the boat. A lunch invitation, good conversation, mailing out the gear I was through with all took time. It was 4:00 pm when I paddled out of sheltered water and into the strait. Fifty miles to the east was the mouth of the muddy Stikine River. High tide had reached there and turned. Seas and wind were pouring back down, reversing a funnel. Grimy dark clouds swirled overhead. Under them, far to the east, was a patch of sun. Not here. Was I really going out there? I was.

At the end of half an hour I'm a mile out from land. I'm also a mile west of where I started, paddling hard on a course north by northeast and being carried west toward

the buoy that marks a ledge. If I can keep it on my left until I pass it, I may be making enough headway. I am paddling 50 strokes a minute. The buoy comes closer, and I can judge my speed north and my drift west. I pass it – on my right. I am between it and Helm Rock, that area marked on the chart as only two fathoms deep. Two miles northeast, the depth is 200 fathoms, but between here and Strait Island the depths are less than 40. All of that 50 miles of water from the Stikine mouth to here is compressing and pouring over these shallows. But these details of depth and distance I find out later when I study the chart. Now, I'm seeing only the surface results.

If I stop paddling, I chance being pushed into the mile-wide Mariposa Reef at the south end of Strait Island, that rocky blue hump ahead. If I turn and go back, I can probably get ashore somewhere near Labouchere Bay, three miles west of where I started. I'll try for Strait Island. Tidal rips and steep waves toss me like a roller coaster. Keep paddling. Pick up the pace.

I need this eight-foot-long paddle to reach beyond my boat's fat, inflated sides, but with a shorter paddle I could stroke even faster. It takes too long to swing this shaft through its arc. The paddle is a windmill, a two-bladed propeller of an ancient aircraft. Chunk and pull. Push the top arm, pull the lower. Could I skirt Mariposa Reef to the south and come up the west side of Strait Island? No, the outgoing tide wraps around both sides of the island and the reef, and I could not paddle against that tide.

I paddle north and move west for an interminable hour. This isn't a green-blue sea. It's a gray glue sea. Now I can see the maelstrom of five-foot breaking surf on the reef to my left. A bell buoy is there, clanging wildly in the breakers. I cannot see the reef, still underwater. The low tide, 3.3 feet, will not be until 9:17 tonight. I scarcely remember the statistics. The small gray book of the tide tables is in the chart bag between my knees. I cannot pause to study it or the chart, but I remember the symbol of a half-sunken wreck on the reef, its symbolic bow canted at a crazy angle.

This boat rides well on the swell. It ships no water, but it was never designed to knife cleanly and swiftly through tide rips. These buoyant round sides bulging out from the hull act as stabilizers to keep it from rocking, but in breaking surf, a wave will lift up one side and capsize the boat. It happened in Hawai'i. The mind races through the thoughts, the machine shoulders never pause. The island sits heavy and dark ahead, details obscured by salt air and clouds.

A diesel tug towing two huge barges is bearing down on me from the east. I glance quickly over my right shoulder. A man stands on the foredeck, watching. At the last minute for them, 100 yards away, they veer to the south to avoid the reef. At least the implied offer of help was there, and I will thank them many times in all the days after. Now, I tell myself what they are probably saying: "Damn fool."

And again, "Damn fool."

And, "You should have gone back while you still could."

And, "You could die."

"Yes, I know."

Strait Island is only a mile away now. Will I reach it, or will the reef claim me, capsizing the boat and tumbling us for a mile through the breakers, the rocks, and the icy water? Can I live through it? I think not. My pace is up to 60 strokes, my heartbeat doubled.

A mass of kelp is south of the island. I see it ahead and paddle madly. Fifty feet to the left, the surf crashes in white breaking seas five feet high. The boat slides into the kelp, a thick ropy mass of stems and blades. Like a breakwater, it calms the seas and holds the boat steady. I grab it in my hands and pull the boat forward, paddle in a patch of clear water between the heavy fronds, pull again, paddle again, and come into quiet water on the lee side of the island.

At a small cove on the southwest corner I go ashore and look for a campsite. Hands together and thank you, gods. I see what looks like bear turd – more like just a splat; I need a scatologist – and thank you very much, gods. I go over to the other side of the shallow pass and find several flat places. It's only 8:00 pm, so there's time to look around and set up camp. Little by little the tension eases. I put up the tent, then go to bed and sleep poorly, with rain and windblown spruce needles dinging on the tarp, and cold seeping up from the ground.

When I awoke, I could tell by the sounds outside the tent that the weather hadn't calmed, and no, I wouldn't leave today. No! I would have to leave by ten o'clock, to get an incoming tide. I looked at the trees lashing in the wind, and out at the whitecaps, and no way! Lethargy most of the day. I walked to the south and found a trickle of a stream for water, if I didn't like the dirty bog by the camp. There must have been a fox farm on the island once, as there were old cabin and cage remains here and at the south cove. Later I'd read in Stephen Hilson's *Exploring Alaska and British Columbia* that a fox farm was here in 1923. I relocate the tarp and camp to the lee side of a big log, write letters, check supplies, and look at charts and maps to confirm the route for the next half of Sumner Strait.

Dinner was beef Stroganoff, four cups of it, but before that I had built a fireplace from cabin debris: an old gray enamel washbasin with the bottom gone, a piece of rusty bucket to replace the bottom, and a scrap of corrugated iron curved around behind the basin and stuck in the ground to reflect the heat. Fed and written and wined, I felt fine. With a fireplace, I didn't mind staying another day. I tried to make the sleeping system warmer, but I needed an Ensolite pad, and hadn't brought one from home because of the bulk.

Friday, I slid out of the bag after nine good hours of sleep. It was still blowing out at the point; I could hear it, but I pulled on my jacket and boots and went over to look. Yes, the whitecaps were still scudding by. Down a bit, maybe to 15 knots. Still a heavy overcast, and the decision was still no. I could get to Sumner Island, two miles west, but I wanted to go north, not west, and I had no desire yet for another battle. Tonight was the last night of my reservation at Devils Elbow, the next cabin, and tomorrow night I was scheduled for Big John Bay. Tough. In three more days, the usual time for storms to die down, I should know this island well. I could build a shelter wall out of the aluminum some trapper had used here for a crude tepee.

In 1915, Daniel Beard wrote *Shelters, Shacks, and Shanties*, and though he kept talking about Boy Scouts and young men, I, a female, found that the book spoke to me like a delightful comrade. I was remembering it now. And what is the hierarchy of small wilderness shelters? A cabin is the highest level, snug, warm, neat, enclosed, with a woodstove. The shanty might be next, crudely built but with an old stove. A hut is less. It has an element of darkness and mystery. It has some kind of kitchen. Witches live in huts and brew potions. Next in disorder is a shack, made of driftwood and old corrugated metal. You'd strive to get it weatherproof. A hovel is the lowest level. You have to crawl in on hands and knees on the dirt floor. A tree house? Ah, there is soaring imagination, wind sighing or roaring in the branches, and a book to read that matches the world of air and leaves. It has a roof or a tarp to keep off the rain. I first read *Master Skylark* in such an aerie in a Kellogg oak tree when I was 10.

Now I built a fire in my fireplace and made a cup of coffee mixed with chocolate. I picked up the journal and read yesterday's account of the day before. The prose wasn't purple, but it should have been – cussing my own stupidity. I stood now on one foot, and then the other, like a blue heron, and alternately kicked each shin with the heel of the other foot. Dummy! Two factors could foul me up on this trip: the weather and my own judgment. One of those I was supposed to control!

Up until two days ago I'd been wearing only the pile pants and jacket, but now I kept the wool underwear on too. Would they be enough 200 miles north in Lynn Canal in September? Most of my thoughts were purely practical: What was going to work here and now? Rarely did I do any contemplation of philosophy one might try in a more secure position. I did ask one question: Who were those gods I was talking to when I landed here?

I'd never believed much in a personal Christian God who sees each sparrow fall. Buddha, Allah, Jesus, Lao-tzu, Kanaloa, Poseidon all seemed to have equal validity. Divinity and personification seemed illogical, though humans for a million years had seemed to need something to worship. Be kind, keep learning, be responsible. It didn't seem necessary to add trappings to that. There seemed to be some power behind the universe – gravity, orbits, stars, our solar system, birth-growth-death, the infinite variety of plants and animals – that kept the natural forces in order and interacting. That was as far as I wanted to go. And I wanted to thank whoever arranged for kelp to grow at the edges of reefs.

The seas were still pouring past at 10:00 am. I opened a red sea urchin for its eggs, and found fat sacs of red roe, but the flavor was not as good as I remembered. James Beard and John McPhee had both written about the edibility of urchin roe, and I remembered uni sushi in Japan. The shallow channel floor here between the two parts of the island was filled with a spiny carpet of smaller green urchins.

Journal, Day 35: Noon now and restless. Have a cup of coffee and go explore. The island covers a square mile of dense forest, uneven bays, and bogs. Half a mile from camp I found an illegible sign nailed to a tree by a tiny stream. Nearby was a mesh wire floor that looked like another fox cage. In the 1920s when red or blue fur stoles were stylish, there were fox farms on many Alaska islands. I remember my aunt wearing a stole of a fox, its small paws hanging over her ample bosom on one side, its head on the other. Styles changed, the price dropped, and now there are only the remains of an industry. I found a 55-gallon gasoline drum tossed up intact on the shore. With the hatchet and a hacksaw I could carve out an opening for an even better fireplace, and make a chimney out of my present reflector metal. You planning to stay a month, Aud? No, but I could. Looked over at Sumner Island and it looks quite possible to paddle to it, across sheltered water in the lee of this island. If I don't get out of here tomorrow I'll consider it.

4:00 pm: Time to take a look at the sea via my path out to the north. The wind sounds are down... Yes, the sea is flat, but it would be six by the time I could pack and leave, and it is high tide at five. I have no need to battle an outgoing tide again. Planning to leave tomorrow at 10:30 am if these seas hold.

Raining now. A strange world in a dream where only the surrounding 50 feet has reality under these misty skies. The temperature is 50 degrees F.

Journal, Day 36, 8:00 am: Half packed and stalling a bit. Takeoff time is half an hour before the low tide of 11:00. That should sweep me along the half mile of the east side of Strait Island into a slack at the northern corner, and then give an incoming tide to push me on. If the wind doesn't come up by then, the theory is OK. Heavy overcast now, and 47 degrees, but with no wind it's comfortable. The fire to dry my socks is out, doused, stirred with my hand. The urchin roe in its red, spiny dish awaits a mink. I'll leave the table counters up, here against the small log, and put the fireplace makings with some dry wood under the big log. Good luck, Aud.

Beef Stroganof

6 large, dried shiitake mushrooms
1 whole onion, chopped
1 tablespoon butter or olive oil
2 packets instant mushroom soup
1 packet dried sour cream
1 cup freeze dried beef, or TVP (textured vegetable protein) or 1 can beef chunks

Soak mushrooms in 1 cup water for 15 minutes. Slice, discarding stems. Save soaking water. Simmer onion in butter or oil. Combine mushroom water withanother cup of water with instant soup and sour cream and add to onions. Adjust thickness. Add beef and mushrooms and heat through. Serve with rice or pasta.

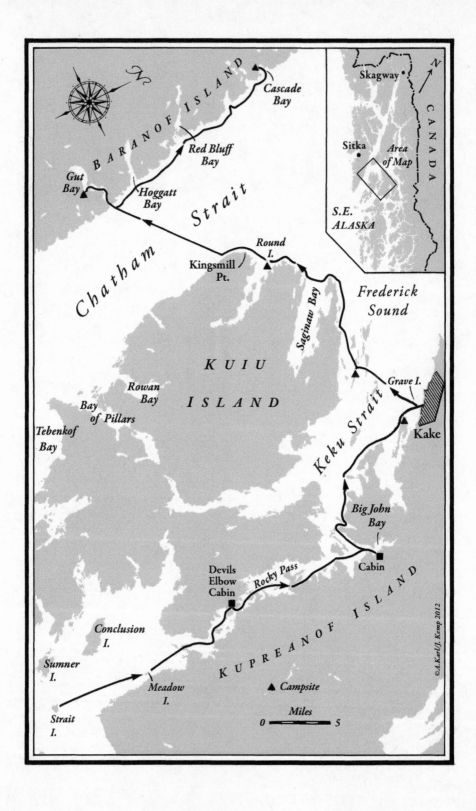

N

BARANOF ISLAND

Cascade
Bay

Red Bluff
Bay

Gut
Bay

Hoggatt
Bay

Chatham   Strait

Kingsmill
Pt.

Round
I.

Saginaw Bay

Frederick
Sound

KUIU
ISLAND

Rowan
Bay

Bay
of Pillars

Tebenkof
Bay

Keku Strait

Grave I.

Kake

Big John
Bay

Cabin

Devils
Elbow
Cabin

Rocky Pass

Conclusion
I.

KUPREANOF ISLAND

Sumner
I.

Meadow
I.

Strait
I.

▲ Campsite

Miles

0   5

©A.KarlfJ.Kemp 2012

Skagway

CANADA

Sitka

Area
of Map

S.E.
ALASKA

N

DEVILS ELBOW TO BARANOF ISLAND

It all worked. At 10 am, I shoved off from Strait Island and in three hours was even with Conclusion Island, where Vancouver completed his northward exploration in 1793, then went back to winter in Hawai'i before returning here the following year. Later I read Vancouver's own journal notes about this area:

> *"On leaving the vessels their* [two small rowboats'] *route was directed toward Conclusion Island, passing in their way thither, a smaller island that lies nearly in the same direction from Point Baker, distant about four miles. This island is low, and is about a mile long in a north and south direction, with a ledge of very dangerous rocks extending from its south point."*

Agreed, Captain Vancouver. I should have read you first.

It was raining, and seals sat on every rock, catching their rest before the high tide covered their perch. A southeast wind made steering more difficult, but at least it wasn't a headwind. During lunch at Meadow Island, I checked the chart, and then headed up past Skiff Island and through a maze of rocks. The seals were keeping up with me for a time, so I sang to them, "I love to go a-paddling, along the ocean track." Each time they surfaced they were nearer, keeping pace only a few yards away, but finally they dropped behind.

A 20-knot wind blew steadily from astern the last two miles. I searched the shore for any sign of the cabin, then rounded an islet and saw the roof of the Forest Service A-frame ahead, right on the narrow isthmus. The Devils Elbow itself, a right-angled narrow tidal pass of roaring rapids, was a mile off to the east. With my shallow draft I had bypassed it via this other route past the cabin.

I landed on the mud just below the grass and began carrying up the first load. Suddenly I was on the edge of a deep pit of fire, 10 feet wide and nearly to the cabin, charring and sparking through the soil, eating back under the turf where it was sheltered from the rain. I spent the next hour carrying seawater to douse it, then stood knee-deep in the wet ashes to throw more buckets of water back under the ledges. Like the peat of Ireland, this is organic soil, the forerunner of coal, and it can burn underground in all directions if a fire is not thoroughly extinguished. Inside the cabin was a small can of apple juice, open and moldy. There were boot prints in the mud and an entry in the cabin's log from 10 days before. The visitors had probably started the fire to burn trash. In a few more hours it would have burned down the cabin.

I woke early to a gray and rainy day. The oil stove wasn't operating, though there was plenty of fuel. Using my vise grips, wrench, and knife, I worked on it for an hour.

The line seemed to be clogged between the carburetor and stove intake, and I couldn't get that section apart. I kept lighting a bit of oil in the stove sump, hoping to dry some clothing still wet from yesterday. I could cook on my small camp stove, but I couldn't warm the cabin with it.

Five more days to the resupply at Kake, where I would need to pare down to the minimum of gear before the next section. That one would be the longest without resupply, and I would also be carrying a pack frame for the planned portage at Catherine Island. My schedule said 16 nights, but it didn't allow for wind, or for resting up after rough days, or for enjoying good new places. I needed to plan on 20 or more. No cabins would be on that leg. The only part of the next three weeks I dreaded was crossing Chatham Strait, 12 miles wide.

So far, the trip had seemed to be more labor and pain and problems than good times. I'd said that five bad days to one good one was a tolerable ratio, but it felt as if it had been ten to one. Four days alone now, and I was standing at the window staring out at the rain wishing for company. I pushed my chin up with one thumb, and went back to evaluating what to send home from Kake. I was remembering that chin-up gesture from a long time back, back to the early days after the divorce: four children, and calluses under the chin.

Hah! I knew what was wrong. I couldn't lay a fire for the next visitor – no wood stove.

In the morning I packed and carried the four loads of boat and gear, plus two spare garbage bags of empty bottles and cans, through hideous, sucking mud up over my boots. Kayakers should leave here at very high tide, or else from the east side of the north cove, where the rocks extend to the water.

In a steady rain, I launched my garbage scow and paddled out to the deepest water I could find on the chart, then sank the cans and bottles, one by one. It's the best system I can figure. Burying doesn't work, as some animal always digs them up. At sea, they're out of sight, and burning the cans first, down on the tidal flat, destroys some of the coating so they'll rust faster in saltwater. My diver friends have agreed with burial at sea, but only if I sink it all 40 fathoms deep, beyond the depth a diver can reach.

I headed north up the pass. It's Keku Strait on the chart, but the local name is Rocky Pass, and for good reason. Buoys or markers were frequent, showing where a boat must turn to avoid a shoal or rocky ledge. The tide was not a problem, and paddling seemed to go so much faster when there was a goal each quarter or half mile.

A year later, all the markers would be gone. The budget of the Coast Guard would be cut, so they would evaluate all the sea routes in Alaska, knowing that not all of the aids to navigation could be maintained and that without maintenance, buoys would drift, lights would go out, and mariners would have no way of knowing which markers were still accurate. All those in Rocky Pass, a route less used than many others, were simply removed. Some things are worth paying taxes for. I'd trade the cost of a few missiles for Coast Guard buoys and markers, the Youth Conservation Corps, a better Tongass National Forest policy, and the Forest Service cabins.

Just ahead was where the tides meet. These places in the middle of a long channel are like a continental divide, where the water flows away to the ocean on each side. Beacon Island had a light that a boat crew could see when coming up from the south or in from the west and know it was the turning point. My chart tersely described the dredged channel there: "5 ft for width of 150 ft April 1966—Conclusion Island, Feb 1977."

I veered off the usual boat route, heading east of Horseshoe Island. Crab pot floats were bright spots in the bay, and pairs of loons came close, but the camera was out of film and impossible to load in the steady rain. One of the most common animals of the whole trip was here, too, one I was unlikely to communicate with: the huge, two-foot-wide orange jellyfish *Cyanea*, which came pulsing by every mile or so. Their tentacles are toxic, and I gave them plenty of room, so as not to accidentally scoop one up with the paddle.

A long tidal flat lay ahead. It was only half an hour to high tide, and I could run out of paddling depth before reaching the Big John Bay cabin. One brief experience in the mud was enough, but there was deeper water off McNaughton Point. Around a spit to the north I looked for likely spots for a cabin, then saw the roof in a clump of trees to the right. Back around and up the slough, marked accurately on the topo map, almost to the doorstep.

On the open slope below the cabin was a field of fireweed, brilliant fuchsia against the lime green tidal grasses and the darker green of the hemlock and spruce. I stood there with a sudden grin, savoring the moment of awareness and color, then hauled up gear and was ecstatic to be there, out of the rain, despite an oil stove with only one cup of oil. This stove worked, and there were 10 gallons of fuel at Devils Elbow where it didn't. Ah well, my clothes would keep me warm, and my own Optimus stove would cook my food.

The pile suit under the foul-weather jacket and pants had been warm enough during the day's steady rain, despite a wet seat (seal that front-fly zipper), cuffs, ankles, socks, and head. I dried off and changed to dry clothes before dinner. After so many years in Hawai'i it was a pleasure to wear a wool sweater. As a shift from dehydrated rations, I ate a can of pork and beans that someone had left here. More sugar than pork, said the label. Then I had a cheese fondue, and hot Jell-O for dessert. Between courses, I made up a glass of Tang with Lemon Hart 151-proof Demerara Rum. *Umm*! Everything is relative. Food I might scorn at home I purr over here.

A mousetrap was in the cupboard, and I set it before bedtime. About 2:00 am it snapped, and, half awake, I lurched over, found the mouse still scrabbling, dropped mouse and trap outside on the deck, and went back to the sleeping bag. In the morning I found the trap on the ground with the dead beastie, wee and thin and sodden from the rain. Once, long before, I had found a nest of mice in a cabin, carried them out to the river that flowed by the door, and tossed them in. One small mouse was still paddling valiantly in the chill water as she disappeared around the bend. Filled with self-loathing, I had gone back to the cabin. No mice scampered over my food and hair that night, but I kept asking, "Did you have a better right to the place than the longtime residents?" and "Mice have a place in the food chain. They eat seeds, convert plants to protein, and are food for the wolves and bears. Are you as useful?"

Now this second arrogant mistake. Communication with endearing creatures is supposed to be one of the themes of this journey. No more mouse murders. Just hang my food. I'll put some cheese and oats outside for them from now on. Nice philosophy, Aud. When I tried it later, it took the mice out to the yard and lured a bear to the doorstep.

Journal, Day 42: Still raining. Fifty degrees now, and indoors without wind it is warm enough. My long underwear pants are Australian wool. They work well, and the top half is ideal, an old cashmere sweater. The boat needs a wash, so I've set it out on the deck to let it partially fill from the rain-gutter spout. I swab it out with the washcloth, empty some water out, deflate it halfway, and swab out the seams. I need a washing machine and dryer or some sun or a stove with lots of heat. I have plenty of fresh saltwater. I could do some writing about this trip while waiting for the rain to stop. In Tahiti once, in a small café, the restroom toilet wasn't working. "Ca ne marche pas" said the proprietor. Ever since, my daughter Noelle and I express doubt by asking, "Will it march?" Can the tender feeling for this country emerge from the physical inconvenience? Will it march?

I was now 20 miles from Kake and the next resupply, a long trip for one day. I had one big meal left, a Spanish paella that called for mussels. Where could I find them in this mud-flat country? At least there was a large cast-iron skillet hanging on the wall. My six-inch-square aluminum frying pan would never march.

I needed binoculars. Flocks of sparrow-size birds were feeding on the muddy shore, running fast, their white bellies showing when the flock wheeled in midair. At noon it was still raining. This was Kupreanof Island I was on. Oh. It didn't make much difference where I was. The only reality was the distance I could see. In the afternoon, I walked south and found mussels for the paella. Tomorrow I'd really have a light load – for one day. The sun came out; it lasted 15 minutes.

I paddled out, looking for the Goldstein Trail, marked on the map – I wondered if hiking this trail would save miles of paddling. I saw a swath through the woods, but it was deep in grass, with logs down across it. Struggling half a mile of it with even one load and I'd be happy to paddle a full day around the other way. Both wolf and bear tracks were on the mud flats near the trailhead. I took photos, comparing the size of my boot print to the bear's paws. Same length, 10 inches. I had a book of animal pawprints, showing the differences between those of grizzlies and black bears.

Back at the cabin I pulled out the recipe for paella by Moira Hodgson in the *New York Times*. It was a combination of chicken and seafood cooked with rice and saffron that I had often made at home. Translating the ingredients into dried or canned items to pack and mail ahead had not been difficult. So now I made up the chicken broth from bouillon powder, stirred in the chopped fresh onion from Point Baker, and added the saffron, those expensive dried wisps of the stigma of *Crocus sativa* that give the whole dish flavor and a yellow color. Someone once said you could get a similar color and flavor using dried marigold petals. I tried it. Ugh! The chicken was canned, and the shrimp, parsley, peas, and bay leaves were dried, but the garlic, lemon, wine, and mussels were all fresh and pungent. The final steaming skillet had juicy mussels in their shells up-ended in golden rice that was slightly crusted on the bottom. Fresh lemon wedges alternated with strips of Spanish pimento across the top. A foil flagon of Australian wine sat next to it, beach asparagus was the side dish, and dessert was apples and blueberries flambés.

I packed to leave in the morning.

Journal, Day 43: It was a much better day. Had I really considered scratching the whole trip and taking the ferry out of Kake? I had. When I was wet and cold and shivering, nothing mattered but getting warm and dry. When I achieved that, the expedition was possible. Warm and dry with sunshine, I would tackle anything.

I left at nine o'clock on an outgoing tide, paddling down past McNaughton Point, hugging the starboard shore. A steady rain lasted past Horseshoe Island, and then, as the big Keku Strait opened up to the west, the rain stopped. Twenty-five miles ahead, across Chatham Strait, were the snowy peaks of Baranof Island. There was no wind and the water was calm. A cabin marked on Entrance Island was gone. Up to Point Hamilton and over to Hamilton Island. No cabin, though one had been marked on the topo. The isthmus was too thick with alder jungle to think of portaging across, so I paddled down the length of the island.

Three teenagers in a skiff came by and told me of the facilities in Kake. Where were the post office, groceries, gasoline? By the end of Hamilton Island I'd made 18 miles. A room and a shower would have been wonderful, but I wasn't up to three more miles and hauling all the gear through town from the dock in search of accommodations.

The campsite I found in a small bight was fine. I checked the high tide time and simply pitched the tent on a *Salicornia* meadow. High tide was within 20 feet, but that was as high as it would be for the next 12 hours. Finish off the paella and off to bed to write the journal.

Whenever I woke during the night it was from some dream of great drama, full of emotional conflict, anxiety, and indecision. Often that just meant I was too warm. No rain. The body woke at six o'clock, and I unzipped the tent and stood up in the opening. The high glaciers over on Baranof were framed between the tips of islands. Off to the right was Grave Island, an ancient burial ground. I could hear the hum of the generators of Kake. I breakfasted, packed, and paddled toward Kake, aiming for the pier of fishing boats.

"Where can I do laundry?" I asked a fisherman.

"Right up there at the cold storage."

Up at the plant I asked again.

"It's for all fishing boat crews."

OK, so I'm a fishing boat, in a small way. I walked in with a high school girl who worked there during the summers. Six dollars an hour to gut, clean, freeze, glaze in ice, and ship the fish. Next year the plant would have its own plane and would be able to fly fish out fresh, get them all the way to Chicago within 24 hours of the time they'd been pulled from the sea. I did a laundry load and took a shower in the women's dressing room, repacked the boat down on the rocks, and paddled on to the main part of town.

Heading in to a small floating dock, I looked for the float where skiffs tie up, as they are the lowest docks to reach up to with my arms and lift myself out of the boat. Shores were easier places to debark, but on floating docks I didn't have the problem of tides leaving the boat stranded or out of reach in deep water. Up at the head of the long pier and a road, I could see a U.S. flag and the green portable building that meant post office.

I tied the boat bow and stern with bowline knots and walked up the ramp. Half of its width was cleated with inch-high wooden strips; the other half was covered with rough sandy decking material for traction. High tide meant an easy slope, but now at low tide the ramp was steeply angled up from its rollers on the floating dock. Coming from Hawai'i with its maximum two-foot tides, this was all a new system. Ingenious.

Striding along the dusty gravel road, I enjoyed walking on level land for the first time since Craig.

"I'd like some General Delivery mail, please. For Sutherland."

"Oh, you're Sutherland!"

The postmaster was happy to get rid of the pile: six packages and 10 letters. I bought supplies and wandered around happily, feeling at ease in this place. As at home in Hale'iwa, I was one of a Caucasian minority. Kake is a native village where the population of about 700 is organized in an effort to provide jobs and good living conditions for all of the residents. I lugged everything down to the dock, where I sorted and stuffed and packed a box to mail home of gear, maps, and charts I no longer needed. Ahead were three weeks and 200 miles of no cabins, no towns, a portage, and the infamous Sergius Narrows.

A fishing boat, the 60-foot *Sea Bound*, slid in along the dock, tied up, and began unloading. The big Tlingit skipper walked over. By now I could predict the conversation.

"Where'd you come from?"

"Ketchikan."

"In that?"

"Yes" with a wry smile.

He looked around for the rest of the expedition, then said, incredulous, "Alone?"

"Yes."

Sometimes the next comments were about insanity, but Sam Jackson knew the sea and small boats, and knew it could be done. He took me aboard, introduced his crew, and gave me instructions for reaching Gut Bay.

"Aim for Mt. Ada. The entrance to the bay is narrow, but if you cross Chatham Strait using the mountain as a landmark, you'll come right into the mouth of the bay."

"Thanks, Sam. You know, you look to me just like the Hawaiians at home."

Sam looked thoughtful. "Maybe I am part Hawaiian. My family is half Haida, half Tlingit, and we have a tradition that some of our ancestors paddled to Hawai'i and returned here centuries ago."

I thought of the 2,000-mile double-canoe voyages between Hawai'i and the Society or Marquesas Islands to the south, dating from the fifth century or earlier, and how even the earliest Hawaiians had legends about a people who had preceded them, a smaller race who built stone walls and fishponds with miraculous speed. There had been a single tantalizing find of skeletal remains on the island of Kaua'i that some scientists had thought showed Asian characteristics. Certainly it was possible. Although I had not heard before of Tlingit or Haida voyages in Hawai'i, I was to hear many more times, here in Alaska and later in British Columbia, of the tradition of a Hawaiian connection. One Tlingit woman said of the voyagers, "Oh, yes. They brought back bamboo."

Eager to be off while the seas held calm, I packed all the gear without really organizing it and shoved off into the placid water, heading for the Keku Islands. Now and then I stopped, let the boat slowly turn, and with a smile inhaled the whole circle of space and magnificence. In a mass of kelp I found a floating Japanese glass ball and took it aboard. I really had no space for souvenirs, but it is impossible to leave a glass ball.

I heard a whale breathe. She surfaced and went down 100 feet to my right. I stopped paddling and waited. Again she came up and blew, about 70 feet behind the boat, then again to my left, about 50 feet away. No flukes were showing as she dove. The last time, I took a photo as her back surfaced, and another as the dorsal fin came up. She was so long that there was time to advance the film between shots. White hide was visible under the mouth. Later I studied the photos and identified her as a fin whale; they grow to a length of 70 feet. She was definitely circling me, and I wondered if it was the yellow color of the boat or the rhythm of the paddle strokes that had attracted all the whales so far.

Rhythms are basic, from the time of the first heartbeat felt within the womb. Footsteps, bass viols, poi pounders, drums, the beat of a bird's wings, the cadence of a crawl stroke – so many rhythms are part of our lives. Was it the paddle pulse or the possibility of a small yellow whale on the surface that had brought this fin whale to meet me? I knew only that I wanted to be swimming in the water with one someday. Roger Payne, in his book *Among Whales*, says that people spook out when they're 10 feet from a whale in the water, and cannot force themselves closer.

I went on with a high sense of well-being, as if I were paddling 10 feet above the water. Small islands were ahead. I passed one with dazzling white beaches, like a South Pacific atoll, then the next one spun me toward it as if magnetized.

These were narrow limestone islands, and I had heard of quarries here. A physical oceanographer could look at my chart, #17368, and make some hypotheses about glaciers, and about sea floor tectonic plate movement, from the elongated northwest-southeast island ridges and the ocean depths. There was so much to learn that I wasn't learning in this steady push for distance, and with only my own data bank for reference.

I paddled in to barely floating depth, braked with the right blade to swing the boat parallel to shore, and swung out a booted leg. I stood up in the shallows and looked around. It felt right. I took the lifeline off my shoulder, lifted the bow of the boat onto the coarse sand, and carried a large rock close enough to loop the line over for a temporary mooring. I walked up to the forest edge, through the tall cow parsnips and ferns, and found a small clearing on the point of the island. It was invisible from shore, but something had said it was there. I went back and carried up the three loads of gear, then the boat.

From the new bottle of wine, which had been wedged in the bow, chilling as I paddled, I poured a plastic glassful, took it and the bottle down to the point, and nestled them in the rocks. The two liquids caught the slanting sun rays, refracting prismatic lights onto the wet pebbles. I went back and set up the tent, returned to the wine, walked back and sorted food, came back to the sea and sat there, sipping wine, eating Camembert and crackers and swiveling to watch the whole scene.

To the east the land was darkening. Night does not fall. It rises from the earth as the sun sinks low, sets, and embraces the land with its shadow. How could I describe this place? Words could only be read and the scene imagined. Even a photo could only be seen. It would not include the sound of the water on the stones, the scent of the spruce trees, the coolness of sea wrack under my hand, or the weary satisfaction of just sitting there after paddling six hours that day, and six weeks before that. The size of these islets and their details of sand, shell and rock beach, grass, driftwood, and flowers, the small woods back of the shore – these are proportioned to kayaks and close-ups, not big cruise ships or ferries. Those get a far outline of the shore, but their only close-ups are of the docks and the towns. This country is made for the pace of a kayak.

Up in the morning to leisurely packing, and to a fresh-food breakfast. I reread all yesterday's mail. The schedule said Kingsmill Point that night and crossing Chatham Strait the next day. The weather might say something different.

People have asked, "What was it like, those long hours of paddling alone?" Each day the first half hour in the boat was full of protest, a feeling of awkward stiffness, and a certainty that I just wouldn't be able to paddle far that day. Slowly the muscles warmed up, the brain became less aware of the body, and the automatic pilot took over, so that the steady rhythmic stroke went on and on like breathing, with no conscious direction or effort. After eight hours, the beat would still be steady and strong.

It was stamina, not muscular strength, that kept the expedition moving.

Ahead there was always a goal. It might be a cove on a far island that I could see only on the chart, one I'd planned to reach when checking the map and chart the previous night. Before I'd be able to find the island, there would first be that far, pale blue point to pass. A darker ridge in front if it was about eight miles away, and before that, there might be the deeper blue-green outline of an islet only four miles away. At two miles I could discern an individual tree; at a mile I could see branches. Fifty yards in front of the boat, a gust of wind would hit the water, riffling it into a crumpled blue tissue, and I'd dig in with the paddle, anticipating the force of the wind. Always I was watching for a swirl of white water or an eddy indicating a rock just below the surface, and all the while my conscious mind was planning the building of a shanty in some hidden cove. Let's see, eight by eight, a shed roof...

The wind stayed low and the paddling was easy, threading through the Keku Islands and crossing Saginaw Bay. En route was the second bear sighting: a black bear, hard to photograph against the dark rocks. A mile later, two humpback whales were leaping and twisting. They mate in the winter in Hawai'i, but this looked like courtship behavior. They separated, and one came toward me, slapping her flukes. I was leery of a bedazzled whale who came straight toward me without circling, and I backed off into a kelp patch until she left.

At dusk I turned into Security Bay and found a spot on Round Islet. There was an 8.5-foot tide when I camped, and it wouldn't be that high again until after nine the next morning, when I would be long gone. I slept warm and dry, and with a small islet's assurance that bears were less likely to be wandering through.

At 5:00 am my internal clock said, "It's time." Cool daylight and a breakfast of oatmeal, but no fluids before the long crossing ahead. I loaded and pushed off. Chatham Strait was quiet, and the spire of Mt. Ada was clear. I pulled out a sheet of lined yellow paper, a letter from Hawai'i I'd received in Kake.

"E ka moana nui, kai hohonu.
E lana malie kou mau 'ale
E ka makani nui, ikaika
I pa aheahe malie 'oe.
O great sea, deep ocean,
Let your waves float quietly.
O great strong wind,
Blow softly and quietly."

I slid the paper into the clear plastic bag. On one side the folded chart showed an inset of the morning's route. By flipping the bag over I could see the topo maps of Kingsmill Point and the edge of Baranof Island – and this incantation. I needed all the mystical power I could touch for the crossing ahead. With such a gentle sea, the 12 miles should have been a four-hour crossing, but my right arm was painful, and six hours was not enough sleep. I sang and stroked, chanted and dozed until the narrow mouth of Gut Bay opened ahead. Once inside, I laid the paddle across the boat and said a soft "*Mahalo*," thanks. I paddled in, marveling at the sheer 1,000-foot granite walls, and at the starfish, each hanging limp by one arm just above the low tide mark. A lopsided smile. They looked the way I felt.

The fifth hot spring of the quest was supposed to be in Gut Bay. "First stream on the north side," said the NOAA and USGS manuals. First from the mouth of the bay or from the head? I wondered, but turned toward the first one in. It was a big alpine creek, splashing down clear and cold through fallen trees and tumbled rocks. I landed and searched. Very cold. I went up a hundred yards and found an eight-foot-deep pool at the base of the long slide of a waterfall. Did it look a bit cloudy in the middle? The scientific way to test it would be with water samples, thermometers, and chemical analysis. Unscientific was to peel off and dive in. It was not hot. I shivered back into my clothes, launched, and paddled south to an island shown on the topo. No landing was possible on the sheer rock sides, but there was a small bay beyond. A stream bounced white riffles into the sea; lupine and high grassy areas indicated a clearing. I checked first for the seaweed and driftwood marking the high tide line, and then to be sure that there were no bear signs, and set up my home.

I was now on the topo map I had been astonished by months before. Of all my maps, this one showed the most contrasts and features, but the reality far surpassed the map. Across the bay the wooded ridges rose to 2,500 feet, but behind me, the gray Matterhorn shape of Mt. Ada was nearly twice that. An icefield came almost down to camp. I could have walked up and chunked ice into my wine glass, but the 38-degree stream was cold enough. I used the awl of my Swiss Army knife to skewer marinated artichoke hearts from their jar.

A powerboat was coming, a sportfishing type, but it went on up the bay, not noticing my camp. If I wanted privacy, maybe I should have hidden the boat, but I usually left it conspicuous, in case I was eaten by a bear and friends had to search for a missing paddler. At 8:30 pm there was another boat, a small sloop under mainsail and outboard, which seemed to be a single-hander, but it, too, went on up the bay.

Gut Bay. By now I realized that *gut* had several meanings, one of which was "a narrow passage or gully as of a stream or bay." Was that where *gutter* came from? I went off to bed to small stream sounds, gurgle, giggle, plink, and a throaty chuckle. I went to sleep laughing. No pressure tomorrow.

During the night I looked out to check the sounds. This was Baranof Island – Russian history, alpine scenery, hot springs – and, along with Admiralty and Chichagof, the other ABC islands, it was also known for grizzly bears.

It lightened into a misty morning, but by ten o'clock the sun was above the shoulder of Mt. Ada, shining bright on the shore across the bay and filtering through the hemlocks and blueberries here. I gave the arm some hot-water-bottle-in-the-sleeve therapy, as I couldn't close my hand when I awoke. Slowly it became more flexible,

though still numb. Maybe it needed soaking in the Baranof Warm Springs. I hoped their tubs were deep ones, not U.S. standard, but they were still 30 miles away.

The single-hander sloop came by again. I yelled and he came in close, so I paddled out, and we exchanged stories. Glen Crum had taught himself to sail on a Montana lake, then put the boat on a trailer to the coast and started a voyage north from Vancouver. We took my canoe aboard and sailed three miles up to the head of the bay. Glen hiked upstream while I caught my first fish of the trip, a three-pounder. It was not until weeks later that I could identify it as a Dolly Varden. Glen came back, admired the catch, and offered to bring a chilled wine to a fish dinner. Yes! Fillets poached in butter, Lyonnaise potatoes, steamed plantain from the shore, mussels in marinade, wine, Hawaiian coconut-haupia pudding with blueberries, and then brandy to toast the place, the sea, the day, and the solo travelers. After dinner I took Glen to his boat, and gave him the glass ball I'd found near Kake.

As darkness rose to meet the coral clouds, I paddled on through a narrow slot just west of my camp, into an inner harbor, a cathedral place in which to talk to the ancient Tlingit gods. Slowly, soundlessly, I moved back to camp, carried up the boat, heated some milk, and sat sipping it, postponing sleep, not wanting this day of sun and glory to end. I came to Gut Bay not knowing what it would be, not knowing it would surpass the map.

Paella Valenciana

2 ½ cups water
3 packets chicken bouillon
2 teaspoons saffron
1 chopped onion
¼ cup olive oil
1 12-oz. hot Portuguese sausage or
    5-oz. can ham or both
4 cloves garlic, minced
1 can Spanish pimento, diced

1 ½ cups short-grain rice
3 teaspoons chopped parsley
1 bay leaf
1 cup dry white wine
2 teaspoons lemon juice
1 cup freeze-dried peas
2 dozen fresh mussels
1 5-oz. can of chicken, shrimp, or clams

Heat water; add bouillon, saffron, and onion. Simmer 15 minutes. In a big skillet, heat oil, add sausage, ham, garlic, pimento. Stir in rice. Add broth, parsley, bay leaf, wine, lemon juice and cook 10 minutes. Salt to taste. Bury in rice a canful of chicken or shrimp or clams or all three. Add mussels so that thier edges will openfacing up. Cover with foil and bake at 325°, or cover and cook on the stove over low heat, until liquid is absorbed and mussels open. Remove foil, decorate with lemon wedges and parsley or fresh wild herbs or Salicornia.

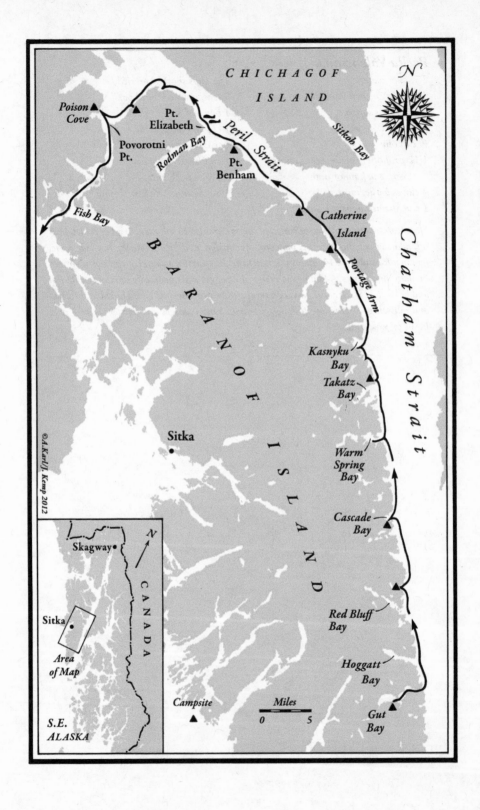

CHICHAGOF
ISLAND

Sitkoh Bay

Poison
Cove

Pt.
Elizabeth

Peril Strait

Povorotni
Pt.

Rodman Bay

Pt.
Benham

Fish Bay

Catherine
Island

Portage Arm

B A R A N O F   I S L A N D

Chatham Strait

Kasnyku
Bay

Takatz
Bay

Sitka

Warm
Spring
Bay

Cascade
Bay

Red Bluff
Bay

Hoggatt
Bay

Campsite

Miles

0   5

Gut
Bay

©A.Karl/J.Kemp 2012

N

Skagway

C A N A D A

Sitka

Area
of Map

S.E.
ALASKA

Warm Springs to Peril Strait

The next day I paddled out of the enclosed alpine peace of Gut Bay and into a headwind. Cove by cove I fought my way north, paused, and fought again. Two miles past the headland of Red Bluff Bay, I pulled out of the wind and into a quiet cove. In the rare sun, a stream ran shallow over flat granite. Yellow marigolds blinked in the grass.

I put the last of the wine to chill in a shaded pool, stripped naked, washed hair, body, and long underwear, and put us all to dry on the warm rocks. Blissfully I sat there and finished a Sunday crossword puzzle, carefully hoarded for a proper moment. I kept watching the whitecapped seas out beyond the cove while my mind played leapfrog.

Up among the trees was a small hollow, like a nest, a place to pitch the tent and curl up for the night, but I felt I ought to push on while the wind was down. Next time you do this, Aud, allow time to stay in good places. Next time! No, I think not. There must be better ways to see this country than 20 percent good stuff and 80 percent bloody hard work and careful survival. A better boat? I didn't know that this wild country would become a passion, that I would come every summer for the next 20 years, in eight different boats, most of them an improvement over the previous model.

By 11:00 pm the sun had set. I had made a few more miles, but the seas and wind were up again. A small cove showed on the topo before Nelson Bay, but an ebbing tide had barred the entrance, so I came ashore on a gravel spit, set up the tent and sleeping bag, left everything packed, and slept. It was possible to do this only when a careful look at the tide table showed that the tide was going out and would not be up to the level of the boat again until I was awake and ready to launch. Even so, I tied the boat on a long line to a rocky crag. Barring tsunamis and bears, I could sleep uninterrupted.

Up at five next morning, and away at six. By seven, the headwind had risen to 20 knots. I toughed it out until 11 am, then came ashore for lunch. A seal kept popping up close to shore and twitching his whiskers. "What is that I smell? Can it be? It is, it is! It's Szechuan eggplant!" I giggled, and he vanished.

Three more hours against the wind and I'd covered the mile into Cascade Bay. A massive cataract of white water drained the high lake system and pounded into the sea, pushing an aerated mass out to form a clear line between the green lake water and the blue salt sea. In the bay to my left was a bit of flat land. I maneuvered in to a narrow shore where there were the fewest barnacles. The tide was outgoing, so I had 20 minutes to check for campsites before the boat would be hard aground. Between two big spruce trees I found an open grassy flat, but was there freshwater? My supply was down to a quart, and it would be impossible to paddle close enough to that huge waterfall. Ah, a trickle of a stream close by. As I came back to paddle the boat around, a river otter slid into the water. Not a sea otter, this was a close relative of Gavin Maxwell's otters in *Ring of Bright Water* in Scotland. The family includes skunk, mink, marten, weasel, and badger. Ten years later, I would paddle in Scotland and walk down to Camusfearna, the poignant site where Maxwell's house had burned, killing Edal, his second otter.

Here in Cascade Bay I built my home: a drift-plank desk propped on two roots of spruce, another drift plank for a kitchen counter, with the bedroom tent beyond them. I sorted through the food sack and decided on a housewarming dinner of cioppino, using fresh mussels from the rocks here. I was hungry enough to want to eat them fast, without shucking each one out of its shell as I ate, so I steamed and shelled them first, using the broth to reconstitute the tomato, wine, and herb sauce that I'd oven dried at home into a leathery slab.

I stayed alert for PSP symptoms, but none appeared, and it was weariness, not poisoning, that staggered the body off to bed for 10 hours of deep sleep.

The north wind on Chatham Strait is up to 20 knots when I wake in the morning. I wait it out: sit and observe cloud patterns, tree forms, grass blades; paddle out into the bay without a load and look up at the high blue glaciers clinging to the spine of Baranof Island; listen to the quiet sounds of this world.

I should travel every other day. Derigging the tent and tarp, packing up the kitchen, carrying gear down to the shore, and packing the boat all takes two hours. Then in the evening two more hours to carry gear, set up camp, fix dinner, and get to bed. It would be better to paddle a long day, come in late, set up just tarp and tent, have just soup, and get to bed. Sleep late in the morning. Have a leisurely day of writing the journal, exploring the woods on shore, studying the chart of the next day's route, resupplying the water, fixing a fine dinner, doing half the repacking, and then early to bed and an early start in the morning.

At noon, a humpback whale was blowing and moving south out in the strait. At two I began packing and at four shoved off, determined to make Baranof's Warm Spring Bay that evening. With the wind down to 10 knots, the six miles took three hours. Five yachts and a big seiner, the *Sea Comber* from Anacortes, in Washington, were there at the small dock.

Warm Spring Bay was just "the way it s'pozed to be." The photo I'd seen in Stephen Hilson's book was true, perfectly proportioned and not distorted by a telephoto lens, which foreshortens the distance. The waterfall was huge and thundering. A former resident had moved away, maddened by the constant roar. Eight hot springs oozed out of the slope; three had been tapped for use, to warm the few houses with steam heat, to make hydroelectric power with a Pelton wheel, and, best of all, to fill hot tubs in a funky old bathhouse.

I inquired at the small general store on a high pier above the floating docks. Two dollars for the use of the bath, two fifty with soap, towel, washcloth, and mat. I had earned the deluxe version and had my choice of a plywood or galvanized tub. The metal one was reminiscent of the childhood round washtub, which I could no longer sit cross-legged in. This was different. Searching for replacements for the old plywood tubs, the owner, Wally Sonnenberg, had come across these in a farm catalog: galvanized horse troughs. Long enough to lie full length, shoulder deep when filled with water, nonmolding, and nearly indestructible: These were ideal. You mustn't turn off the hot water, a sign warned, because compression steam would burst the pipes. The drain was a two-foot-high hollow plastic pipe. When the water was more than two feet deep, it simply overflowed down the inside of the pipe.

I soaked and steamed for an hour, then, clean and limp and blissful, walked the trail up to the lake and back. At dinner aboard one of the yachts, the crew gave me doomsday predictions of the impossibility of this voyage on which I'd already paddled 400 miles. Yachtsmen seldom really comprehended boats this small, with neither sail or motor. Not until the following year did I stay long enough to better know and appreciate Wally and to meet Ben Rowely, the gentle 80-year-old carpenter who lived on his boat and did jobs throughout southeast Alaska. Then, too, I met Curtis Rindlaub from Connecticut, who was paddling south from Glacier Bay. We exchanged campsite information, north for south.

It was getting late. At 10:00 pm I said good-bye and paddled down the bay. In the first cove, a house occupied the only flat ground. In the second, a crunched cabin took up the space. I went on, no campsites, so just kept paddling out of the bay into the night. There were oily swells, but no wind. By flashlight I checked the topo map and chart and plotted a compass course. No offshore rocks or reefs. Keep paddling. By midnight it was too dark to see the water, but I could make out the outlines of the 2,000-foot-high mountains to my left. A wave lifted the boat. OK, so there's a bit of a swell. It's not breaking at the top or I'd see the phosphorescence and the white water and feel the wind. Keep paddling. Something bumped the boat hard. It's just a log; you've hit them before. There's nothing out here you don't already know. A big splash? Just a seal. I was eating from a bag of chewy candy from the little store and thinking,

> "Out of the night that covers me,
> Black as the pit from pole to pole,
> I thank whatever gods may be
> for black licorice."

Finally, by 4:30 am, I could read the map and chart, and figured by the mountain contours and the coves that I was past Takatz Bay. To my left was a landing beach. Ready for sleep, I pulled in, carried up the gear and then the boat, and set up the tent as a refuge from bugs.

Across a stream, a dark animal, bigger than an otter, with a thick, furry, blond-striped coat, looked at me and unhurriedly, disdainfully, walked into the forest. A red squirrel chattered and ran toward me. Was I a refuge, a better choice than the other animal?

When I awoke three hours later, ready to paddle again, there were parallel scratches on the side of the boat where I had laid a smelly bait herring two weeks before. Later I checked photographs in Alaska Geographic's book of mammals, and found that my bushy animal was a wolverine, who has a reputation, shared with the tiny shrew, as the most ferocious animal, pound for pound, in the world. A wolverine's fur is valued for its durability, not for its mythical quality of being frost-repellent.

The tide would be high in another hour, and Portage Arm, where I needed the high tide to cut down the carrying distance across the isthmus, was still nine miles away. At least I had the high to launch with now. Around a curve I passed Waterfall Cove, hearing its roar back in the cleft. Just past Ell Cove was a pearly sand beach that swung me hard left to a tiny shore, 30 feet wide and U-shaped. The rocks on its sides were quiet sphinx paws, furry with black moss, and the head and body of the rock beast wore a matted coat of flattened crowberry – so like our Hawaiian mountain plant that I laughed, "Hello, pukiawe. Nice to see your relatives here."

Trudging on the fine sand was like walking on sugar: the only place in Alaska I've ever seen such a beach. Across eight miles of the pale blue Chatham Strait was the darker blue of Admiralty Island, with everlasting snow on the ridges. Admiralty has one grizzly bear per square mile. I paddled on into Kasnyku Bay to check out the "abandoned lighthouse" marked on the chart. It was outhouse-size, not big enough to use as a shelter cabin.

A skiff came powering up to check me out. Back in a corner of the bay was the modern Hidden Falls salmon hatchery, which the staff proudly escorted me through. I felt grubby and out of place in this world of chrome, plastic, steel, motors, and flush toilets. I took the crew's recommendations for campsites and paddled on.

That evening I found a good spot. At sunset I gathered mussels, the giant *Mytilis californianus*, tearing them loose from the byssuses, the threads that held them to the rocks. They were rare this far north. Had we really called them horse mussels years ago in Southern California and only used them for bait? The middle-sized ones were more tender than the seven-inch-long monsters. I made a fire on the beach of driftwood and dead alder sticks, let it burn down to coals, then covered it with a thick layer of fucus. I scooped a nest for the mussels and covered them with more of the seaweed. While waiting, I unpacked the sleeping bag and fluffed it, inflated the air mattress, and laid them inside the tent.

I minced garlic into the smallest pot, put in a chunk of butter, and laid the pot on top of the steaming seaweed. I brought the chilled bottle of wine from the stream, undid the seaweed nest, lifted out each opened mussel and dipped it into the garlic butter. Ah! The smoked, steamed flavor, the taste, smell, and texture of the mussels, the sounds of the sea, and the deep colors of the sky – all five senses were melded in a rich evening harmony.

A day later, just before high tide, I paddled to the east end of Portage Arm. Both chart and topo map indicated a water route through the isthmus, but it did not exist.

Not even the highest tide would connect a waterway through the bogs and logs. When the weight of the glaciers over all this land for centuries was gone, the land began rising. Isostatic rebound, the geologists call it.

I tied up the boat and walked to higher ground, scanning ahead for the best route. A neatly trampled path led through the grass. How nice! Oops. I bent a knuckle into the pile of bear crap. Cold. At least she hadn't been here within the last hour or two, but from the turd size it was probably not she, but a large he. Sing loudly, Aud, as you portage. How about that old French song that sounds like a crew of voyageurs? Lustily, now:

"Chevaliers de la table ronde,
Goutons voir si le vin est bon…"

I picked up the boat and carried it on my head, with a loaded pack frame on my back. The trail disappeared to the right into the woods, so I bushwhacked over logs, through shoulder-high fireweed and cow parsnip, singing loudly, to a point by a spruce tree where I could see water ahead. Two more trips took me through all the verses of "Chevaliers," all the parts of plucky "Alouette," and several repetitions of the mournful end of the jolly swagman in "Waltzing Matilda." Any bear would have fled by now at full gallop.

By the time all of the gear was down to the water again, the tide was in full retreat, too. I would carry a load to a point, and by the time the other bags had been brought there, the water had receded. Leapfrogging loads, I finally caught up, piled the bags in, and then, in water too shallow to float the boat with me aboard, hooked the lifeline to the bow and started towing, wading through the shallows. I was glad that I hadn't deflated the boat. In the five minutes it would take to pump it up again I would have lost the tide.

At 10:00 pm I came out of the inlet and went along the south shore to get water from a creek, then over to Dead Tree Island. Three cabins were on the topo map, but as usual, none remained. It was windy and cold. I paddled on to Eva Bay for the night.

In the morning's first sleepy reconnaissance I could see the two-mile-wide entrance from the north-south Chatham Strait into the east-west Peril Strait. It separated Chichagof Island to the north from Baranof Island behind me. I had bypassed the usual ferry and small cruise ship route by angling through Portage Arm.

A skiff was drawn up on shore a half mile away, with only one slim person walking about. Curious, I came across, and we compared notes as soloists. Ted was 18, and he was celebrating his first summer out of school by seeing as much as he could of Alaska in a month. He used a 14-foot skiff with a small motor and tied the heavy boat on shore at high tide each night, then set up his tent. Hmmmmm. A lot could be said for motors, especially against headwinds. He couldn't portage the isthmus, so would be heading east around Catherine Island. We exchanged campsite information, and I paddled on west into a 15-knot headwind. I made one mile in an hour and a half.

Just ahead, a stream was on the chart. I came ashore saying, "Well, I may be here for a while. May as well find a good campsite." Though the wind made travel nearly impossible out on Peril Strait, the day was pure sunshine, the fourth whole day of it so far in the 85-day trip.

Tucked back in the trees was a clearing. By 11:00 am I had built a kitchen counter at stand-up height by placing a drift plank across the limbs of two small spruce trees. Drift plywood made a table for dining and library. The tarp made a windbreak wall, the tent was set up for the bedroom, and the wine from the Warm Spring's store, the juice, and the cheese were chilling in the stream. The laundry was hung to dry, and a piece of seiner netting from the beach provided a hammock, as I'd sent my small one home.

I lay bare in the sun, listening, dreaming, melting like a lighted candle into the earth. It was strange to see my bare feet again. They usually went from boot to bed to boot again, without taking off the socks. They looked quite fragile. My hands, however, are tools – pliers, carabiners, vise grips, antennae, turnbuckles. I should spray them with Rustoleum. No sense trying to grow long nails or putting on polish. Only my toenails are painted pink.

Every hour I'd walk out and look northwest. I could see eight miles – of whitecaps. This was Peril Strait at its loveliest for a sailor in a sloop or ketch going east, but not for me, a paddler with an inflatable canoe going west. The wind continued at a steady 15 to 20 knots.

I was musing about the use of the words *canoe* and *kayak*. In Hawai'i I had always called my boats canoes. *Wa'a* is the Hawaiian word for canoe, and it is the indigenous craft, adze-carved from a log and balanced by an outrigger or another hull. In northern Alaska and Greenland, the kayak had evolved – a narrow, fully decked hunting weapon to carry the hunter and his spear within range of a seal or walrus. Now I was in Alaska, but not in kayak country. This was the southeast, where Tlingit and Haida had paddled single-hulled, undecked, adzed boats. My plastic inflatable needed a new word. Until it was coined, I'd continue with both *canoe* and *kayak*.

Dinner was a tuna-rice casserole, chablis, and a salad of beach asparagus and goose tongue from the gravelly point beyond camp. Dessert was apple Betty made from stewed dried apples with a granola bar crumbled on top. After dinner I had tea with rum: an affinity there. I might be holed up here for three nights, as on Strait Island, but now I had a stream and at least one day of sunshine.

There is a rhythm to this country: hard paddling and rest, rain and sun, wind and calm, high tide and low tide. A sense of space and the far-off throb of a diesel tugboat. A forest enclosure and the chirp of a tiny brown bird. People and a sense of being human, then a week of being a solo animal in an animal world. A dozen dragonflies hovering, then soaring out of sight. The mite of a red spider crawling over my toe. Strange that I kill mice and carefully move spiders.

At 8:00 pm the temperature was a pleasant 53 degrees in the shade. If I'd had any thought of night paddling, I dropped it. The seas were still whipping by at 20 knots. Under my elbow as I wrote, the space was filled five inches deep with pieces of spruce cones that a squirrel had carefully shredded. Pine nuts from piñon trees I knew, but spruce nuts? The mind was reluctant to let go of the day, but the body said it was time to sleep.

I woke at four o'clock and from the tent door saw the trees bending in the wind. At six I went stomping out to the shore in boots, jacket, and long underwear. Wind. OK, back to bed and slept until eight, then up to a cloudy sky. A ferry came up the strait from the northeast, timing the tide to get the noon slack at Sergius Narrows. Coffee to warm my hands. How different the mood when there is no sun. It's about 24 miles to Poison Cove, my next goal. One day of tailwinds, two normal days, and who knows how many of this kind.

A leisurely breakfast of an omelet with a topping of crumbled bacon, smoked salmon, and onions. By 10:30 am the sun was out briefly, and my morale was back in high gear. Even against the wind I should be able to make the seven miles to Rodman Bay.

Getting into the boat for takeoff was always a precise maneuver. After everything was stowed and the boat afloat, I'd take the end of the lifeline off the anchor rock and loop it over my shoulder. From the left side always, like getting on a horse, I'd swing up my booted right foot, shake off the water, put it across, sit carefully in, then swing up my other foot, let it drip, and place it on the gunwale. Only in Alaska, where there was such quiet water on the shore, could I do such a neat takeoff. In Hawai'i, where the surf was usually breaking, it was always a system of timing the wave sets for a lull, throwing the body into the boat, and paddling madly before the next wave crashed. No precision, just get the hell offshore.

An incoming tide, an outgoing wind, and five hours of paddling got me to the edge of four-mile-deep Rodman Bay on the south side of Peril Strait. There was a small beach and a clearing, with the sun coming through an old partially logged area to the south. There was no creek, but I had brought three quarts in the water bag, which still smelled faintly of the wine it used to hold. On shore was a bundle of 23 logs strapped together. In the parlance of logging, the specific name really is *bundle*, I found out later. Across the strait was a logging camp, and False Island, a Young Adult Conservation Corps camp. I sat on a rock at the edge of my clearing and looked out. A sailboat went by, main and jib raised, making good time. I wondered where they would anchor, or if they would sail all night.

I awoke at 5:00 am to solid fog with 50-foot visibility. I unfolded the chart and figured a compass course. Point Benham to Point Elizabeth, 280 degrees uncorrected, 252 degrees corrected, allowing for an easterly compass variation of 28 degrees. My course was often zigzag in this rudderless boat, but there was no wind. I was powering the stroke and figured two hours for the four miles. I overcorrected the course a bit so as to hit land and then turn right, rather than err to the right and keep going up the strait for miles in the fog.

In less than two hours trees appeared suddenly in the mist. As happy as a navigator seeing land ahead after crossing an ocean, I turned right and rounded Point Elizabeth while the sun burned through the fog, then clouded over again. Another two miles, and I saw a huge rusty winch on the shore. Was it from some shipwreck or from an old logging camp? I paddled toward shore to see it closer and to make a pit stop, but I was floating on something solid – fish.

I secured the boat, rigged the pole, and cast out. Ten casts brought me a five-pound humpy salmon. Five more casts brought an eight-pounder. By now I was wearing boots full of water from wading out deeper than my boot tops to unhook the lure from the kelp. Could I have gone ashore and peeled off the socks and trousers first? Of course, but one does not always act rationally when converted from gentle paddler into mighty predator. At least the $36 for the nonresident fishing license had paid off. Cleaning the fish, I found that both had eggs. Ah, caviar for the morning omelet.

En route again, I met and talked with a friendly couple aboard the *Skookumchuck*, a ketch from Seattle. I was so bedazzled I forgot to offer one of the fish. Around Nismeni Cove was a small stream, a good place to cook dinner. I filleted the smaller fish and had two big slabs of meat. The grill was scarcely large enough for this size of beast, but I cut chunks, swabbed them with butter and shoyu, and kept pushing alder coals under the grill. I dipped the red roe into boiling water for a few seconds, then scraped the eggs from the membrane, salted them lightly, and bagged them.

An hour later, full, I waddled back to the boat and paddled away from the kitchen site, wondering why *waddled* and *paddled* don't rhyme. Thoughts of bears were always there. I should cook and eat at one place, sleep at another when I'm wafting odors of salmon.

Two big ferries have gone by today. I'm right on their route and their radar wouldn't pick up this PVC plastic boat, but I'm safely hugging the shore and out of their way.

Just past Rocky Point I found a camp spot, drank hot milk with brandy, studied the topos and the charts, and recalled all the advice for Sergius Narrows, two days from now. Three miles ahead a ferry came out from behind Povorotni Island, indicating the route.

I put the second fish into a heavy double-folded plastic bag, then weighted it with rocks in a stream pool to refrigerate. Building a smoke oven to preserve it could be a full day's project. I went off to bed in a dry tent – there'd been very little rain for two weeks.

Breakfast was salmon poached in butter and the caviar omelet. Plenty of protein. I felt like some Russian czarina, but they never got to Alaska. Are there salmon in Russia, or did Catherine the Great have only sturgeon-roe caviar? The Japanese now have red *ikura* on their sushi, imported from Seattle and Alaska. But Aleksandr Baranov – manager of the Russian-American company that established a fur trade based in Sitka, who built a "castle" on the most prominent waterfront hill and after years of hardship finally furnished it with luxuries from Europe and Asia – surely Baranov found that the little bubbles of salmon caviar burst in your mouth with intense flavor.

A big tug with a barge was heading toward Sitka. A 400-foot ferry would be difficult enough to get through the angled route of the narrows, but a barge on a tow line cuts corners like a trailer. Ah! The tug paused and shortened the towline, winching it in so that what was three tug lengths between them was now less than one. It disappeared around Povorotni Island as I packed and launched.

I angled over to Poison Cove to see if a cabin marked on the topo was still there. In 1799 a team of Baranov's men, hunting for sea otter furs, camped in the cove – a colorful group of small agile Aleuts in their skin kayaks, fierce local Tlingits in cedar log canoes, and burly Russian overseers. They are said to have feasted on mussels, and over 100 men died from the effects of a "red tide."

Now the cove was filled with floating logs, tightly corralled and waiting for a tug to haul them out. The cabin was there and occupied by Paul and Susan Hennon, who were doing research on the cedar trees. Throughout southeastern Alaska, cedars had been dying; in some forests, every bare tree was a dead cedar. The Hennons were investigating: checking aerial photos back to 1927, making microscopic examinations of live and dead tissues, collecting fungi, and doing root excavations of live, dying, and dead trees. They were especially trying to find if this was a problem caused by humans.

It was my first long conversation, except with myself, since Gut Bay. We talked with the ease of old friends about fungi and hot springs, botany and history, food and fishing. They had been at Poison Cove since June, and were coexisting with the brown bears that seemed to live across the cove. As I walked back along the shore to my campsite, I checked the sand carefully for pawprints. So far on the trip I had seen two black bears from afar, but it was the brown bear, the grizzly bear, who had the well-deserved reputation for an unpredictable temper; for attacking and chewing up people; in short, for most of the gruesome bear stories that are told everywhere in Alaska. *Ursus arctos*, formerly *horribilis*: a creature of nightmares that come true.

At six in the morning I sorted maps, packed, and carried gear to the boat. Neatly imprinted in the sand were bear tracks that had not been there the evening before. They led up to the edge of the forest, 30 feet from the tent, and then went back along the shore, past the cabin, toward the other side of the cove. It was reassuring to think of a bear on an evening stroll, simply coming to check out a new scent, and then returning on her usual route. Still, how far had she come padding into the forest on the soft duff where I could not see her tracks? Did she sniff at the tent screen, a foot from my head?

Bear Bars

1 18-oz. jar chunky peanut butter
1½ cups honey
1½ cups or more powdered skim or whole milk (not instant)

Mix together into a stiff dough. Add nuts, raisins, or chopped dates if desired. Pat firmly into two nine-by-nine-inch pans. Cut into bars or squares. Wrap each piece in foil. Pack in ziplock bags. Make and wrap at home no more than two days before departure. Make them too far ahead and you'll eat them all before you go.

Two of these every day for lunch, plus dried fruit, fruit rolls, nuts, gorp, granola bars, and juice or water will keep you paddling.

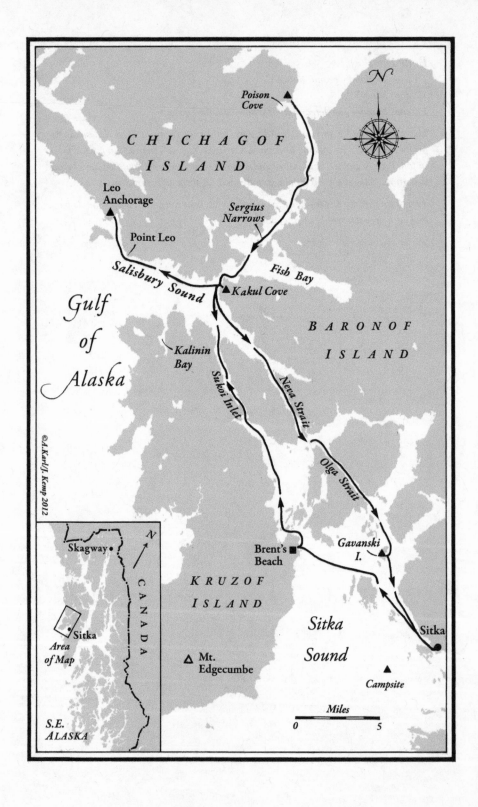

SERGIUS NARROWS, SITKA, AND NORTH

Today, on a detour south to Sitka for a resupply package, I would go through Sergius Narrows, the most infamous passage in all of southeastern Alaska. The NOAA Coast Pilot, normally calm and restrained, turns to comparatively livid prose to describe the Narrows: "At the strength of the current the water is very much disturbed, heaving up over West Francis Rock, Prolewy Rock, and Wayanda Ledge in the middle, and boiling and swirling in the channel ..." The Alaska Geographic southeast issue shows photos of a red, eight-foot-tall, one-ton, anchored channel buoy being pulled completely underwater by the run of the tide. In nine miles, I would be there.

Months before, an oceanographer and I had calculated that the correct time to arrive at the Narrows was at high slack, but now a headwind had put me behind schedule. I picked up the pace; the wind picked up also. Middle Point to Mountain Head, and then toward Pinta Head, comparing the landforms that I could see ahead to those on the topo map and chart in my lap. I was on the south side of the slot. I looked north, past Rapids Island, over to the red buoys that marked the boat passage through Sergius Narrows. There was a loud roar like a waterfall, but the sound wasn't the Narrows; it was rapids, boiling over the rocks just 50 yards to my right. Beyond them was Canoe Pass, too shallow for larger boats but just right for Indian canoes.

It was an hour past high tide, not the slack that I was supposed to use, which occurs here two hours before the high at Sitka. The book of current tables said I now had a seven-knot current. I needed to add some paddling speed of my own in order to have steerageway, but the current was squirting me through. Dodge the rocks, use the current, watch the kelp streaming my way. How rare to see the land going by so fast with so little effort. A lot can be said in favor of rivers. They flow.

Past the Narrows the current slowed, and I headed for Range Point against the wind. Up the long length of Fish Bay to my left was another item on my hot springs project. It would take six miles of paddling to the shoreline trailhead – if I could find it. Four miles of walking to the hot springs streams, through "thick bears," Ted at Eva Bay had said. Yes, even one 600-pound, murderously efficient grizzly is thick. Then four miles walking back to Fish Bay plus six miles paddling back to this point against the wind. I'd just have to wait until Sitka to get reports on the status of Fish Bay hot springs.

At Kakul Narrows were more rocks and a red buoy, marking a ledge with strong currents on each side.

"One side or the other, Aud. Not dead center."

At 10:00 pm, I looked at a small cove for a camp. Instinct said, "Next one."

The shoreline looked like Monterey and Carmel in California, with jagged rocks and trees stunted from the wind like bonsai in a Japanese garden. I swung left, into a narrow kelp-choked entrance just opposite the Kakul lighted buoy.

I gasped. A sand beach curved inside the rock-gate entrance. There were two tiny creeks, flat places for a tent, and a view of all the boat traffic going in and out of Sergius Narrows. To the northwest were the mountain cliffs edging Salisbury Sound, the route north that I'd be following next week. For now, I was detouring south to Sitka for a resupply package.

On the low tide it was a long haul up the beach. Two loads on the pack frame with a bag in each hand, then back for the boat, with its pump and repair kit wedged in the bow, the paddle and water bag stuffed in the stern. Twenty-three pounds in a box or a bag that I can heft onto a hipbone shelf is an easy carry. Twenty-three pounds of child with armpits that I can grab to throw the squirmy, giggly mass up onto a shoulder is an enjoyable load. But after a 12-hour working day, 23 pounds of windblown boat and gear with no handles is an awkward load, requiring numerous grunts through clenched jaws to get up the steep slope of a beach.

I set up the tarp and tent, then made instant mac and cheese and miso soup and gulped them down, grateful for the spreading warmth in the belly. A half ounce of brandy went down smoothly, and it was nearly dark. I slid into bed, figuring that a grizzly could gnaw me down to the knees before I woke up.

On a minus tide next morning the cove was nearly dry. In knee-high boots I walked across. A two-pound octopus was there in the shallows. I had my knife and thought about dinner, but she belonged there. I stroked her between the eyes and she pulsed under my fingers. Another area for camping was on the far side, without a water supply but with a good cast-off oil drum. With tin snips and a hacksaw I could create a stove. Maybe I should start carrying stovepipe along. Everything had to do double duty; what other uses could I find for some three-foot-long metal cylinders?

This place had been used before and mistreated. I took two garbage bags of cans and bottles out with me to the 60-fathom line, and sank them one by one. There must be some immutable law of physics which states that it is possible to bring into a camp by plane or power boat at least 50 pounds of bottles and cans per person, but that it is not possible to remove them when empty by the same plane or boat upon departure. Law two: Glass or metal not carried out must not be piled or left intact, but must be smashed and scattered. But this place was worth the cleanup, and I've told other boaters about it.

A tailwind, a lovely endearing tailwind (you get pretty gooey about tailwinds after days of beating into headwinds), plus the incoming tide gave me a pleasant paddle down Neva Strait, named after the world-circling Russian ship. The Neva gave her Captain Lisianski and Aleksandr Baranov good service; then, in January 1813, after a four-month voyage from Russia, she was wrecked in a storm only 17 miles from

Sitka. Pitiful bodies of women and children washed ashore on the southwest corner of Kruzof Island.

On tiny Highwater Island, in the middle of the Strait, were the crunched remains of a cabin on a steep slope. What a view they must have had, right into all the ferries and tugs from 100 feet away. But no, the marine highway of ferries began only in 1960 with one small boat, the *Chilkat*. The details of this cabin looked as if it dated back to the 1920s. I wondered if the owner had rowed a small skiff to Sitka to get his supplies, just as I was doing.

In Olga Strait the tide turned against me, the tailwind was gone, and it was a fight from there on to the Gavanski Islands and a wakeful night of animals clattering on the shore rocks. Dimly I decided it had to be deer. Bear paws wouldn't clatter. The sky lightened into a rainy morning with a long six miles ahead into Sitka. I was ready for a bed, a bath, a roof, and fresh food.

A boy fishing on the rocks called out. Not "Where ya from?" but "Where are you out of?" so I could reply in proper clipper-ship fashion, "Eight weeks out of Ketchikan, bound for Skagway."

With 8,000 people, Sitka was my first big town since Ketchikan. I paddled past a forest of fishing-boat masts up to a small dock, tied up, slid out of the bib pants, and walked up the ramp. I was aware of my boots and dirty foul-weather jacket, but a glance around showed that I matched the local style. The tourists from cruise ships looked clean and neat in their London Fog raincoats, but many of the rest of us were from fishing boats or log camps, and grubby was normal.

The Sheffield Hotel wanted $54 a night, the Shee Atika was first class and the same price, but the Sitka Hotel was $29, and they didn't blink when I hauled in a rolled-up, wet boat. The post office had my resupply box and a dozen letters from home. The café pizza was worth the five dollars it cost. I brought a bottle of chilled Mondavi chardonnay and the pizza back to the room, sat on a real chair instead of a log, put my feet on the window sill, and read mail while watching the street scene in Sitka.

Excavations out on the street for a new sewer line had unearthed a wooden well from the old Russian days. It had been photographed, measured, and viewed by all the sidewalk superintendents, and would soon be buried again as the job was completed. I took a long hot shower, and then, on the back of a map, I wrote a blurry, wine-stained note of self advice and posted it on the wall: "You've been battering your body long enough. Sleep!"

The young doctor I saw the next day wasn't certain about my right arm. Neurological tests came out OK. Rest, pain-killers, and more rest were prescribed, so for three days I went shopping and sightseeing, learning about the area.

Sitka suited me. It was about as small as you could get and still have the five things a town needs as a place to live: 1. A community college to take or teach classes. 2. A good public library. 3. A National Park for access to the knowledge of the naturalists

and historians. 4. A warm-water swimming pool. 5. A thrift shop. Use money for plane fare, boats, and good wine, not for clothes and oddments you can buy second-hand. My "TS principle" isn't Eliot or Tough Shit, it's Thrift Shops.

Sitka also has a varied history. Ellen Searby and Henry Jori's helpful guide, *Alaska's Inside Passage Traveler*, sums it up:

> "Sitka was the site of the first Russian settlement in Southeast Alaska, established by Baranof in 1799. Originally located just north of where the ferry terminal now stands, it was wiped out by Tlingit Indians. A new fort and town were built at the present townsite. For several years Sitka was the European cultural center of the Pacific. American, Spanish, and British ships came here to trade with the Russians for otter pelts. When the United States bought Alaska from the Russians in 1867, the changeover took place in Sitka. Her Russian heritage, her historic sites and buildings, the Sheldon Jackson museum (with its excellent Indian collection), and the Sitka National Historical Park make a stopover here very rewarding."

It felt good to walk again, striding along in running shoes instead of climbing over kelp-covered rocks in boots. I bought six pounds of fresh groceries, the usual: onions, lemons, butter, fruit, cheese, and wine.

At Observatory Books the conversation was books, mostly old and used. We weren't much interested in new ones or best sellers, except for John McPhee's *Coming into the Country*. Dee Longenbaugh, the owner, commented about book choices. The office-job people who came in for reading material wanted something lightweight at night. The fishing population who lived on their boats came for Dostoyevsky, Kafka, and Tolstoy. Accustomed to days of physical exhaustion and rough seas, they wanted something deep and real.

The Old Harbor Bookstore was another great place to browse – all the books I needed in the boat for reference as I traveled but had no space for. It also had the three volumes of Captain George Vancouver's journals. Vancouver has never been given enough credit for his extensive exploration and careful mapping of this whole coast-line. No motors, just oars in small boats, using the big ship with its awkward square sails as a base, fearful of fierce Native Americans, forced south by icy storms each winter, but returning each spring to endure it all again. Years later I read Jonathan Raban's *Passage to Juneau*. Vancouver evidently did not engender the fierce loyalty that sailors gave to his former captain, James Cook.

Goddard, the eighth on the list of hot springs along my route, was 20 miles south of Sitka. I asked about it, was told how popular and crowded it usually was, and decided to save it for another year. I asked also about the Fish Bay springs. Forest Service personnel who had been there described it as a warm, muddy bog.

Three days of town were enough, and I headed northwest to Brent's Beach. It was so good to be back in the woods and alone that I went around exclaiming over each blueberry and newly sprouted mushroom. There was a long black-sand beach to run on, but the Forest Service cabin, like Amargura near Craig, was too accessible to town, and difficult to maintain. There were no tools or wood supply, though someone had brought a barbecue grate and a giant cast-iron griddle.

I repaired the oven door and put the roof back on the outhouse, but couldn't do much about the cabin. The shakes had been pounded directly into the plywood A-frame walls without any furring strips, so all the nails came through; it was like living inside a nest of porcupines. Forest Service people had said that the cabin was started by a father as a memorial to his son, who had drowned near here. Would a small plaque explaining that origin prevent the use of the cabin for target practice? Would a big wallboard of cedar or soft pine and a sign saying "Carve names and initials here" help the walls and tables? Probably not. That cabin has since been replaced by a neat little cedar one in Pan-Abode style.

Away next morning at nine o'clock. When I checked my wrist for time I remembered what Heather, one of my best paddling buddies, once asked: "How is a generation raised on digital watches going to know how to turn a set screw clockwise or counterclockwise?"

Up with the tide through West Channel and the Magoun Islands, then past Mud Bay. How many Mud Bays are there in southeastern Alaska? Probably a dozen with the name and a hundred more with the mud. Up Sukoi Inlet, parallel to Neva Strait farther east. It was 20 minutes before an eight-foot high tide, and I slid through the narrows without needing to portage.

In another half mile, fish were thick in shallow water. I paddled to shore, cast out, and caught one five-pound humpy salmon and then, in five minutes, another. One to eat and one to trade or smoke was enough. I was debating whether to cross Salisbury Sound, swing left to Kalinin Bay, and camp on the Scraggy Islands, or go back to my small cove by the Kakul light. Swells and surge were coming in from the open sea out to the west. Scraggy Island had a sand beach, but the entrance was just a boat width, and if the surf came up I'd be stuck there.

I paddled over to my cove and saw smoke. I edged the boat in, figuring that if I saw a power boat, I'd leave, but it was a group of six kayakers in Folbots, from Harvard Medical School in Boston, who insisted that I was setting a precedent and that they would expect an inflatable yellow kayak to deliver fresh fish each evening for the rest of their voyage. At sunset we laid out the buffet: chowder, grilled salmon, salmon baked in foil, and steamed clams and cockles, plus one of the easily carried California boxed wines.

Next morning I again launched the garbage scow, paddled into the surge and kelp, then jettisoned the cargo. Out past Gogloi and Round Islands, the swells of Salisbury Sound kept increasing until they were eight feet high, but they were gentle billows, with no wind to blow the tops off, just rising, lifting the boat, then passing under me and away. In three hours I rounded Point Leo, and then the other kayakers caught up.

123

Four paddle blades per boat gave them twice the speed. We all went into the quieter waters of Leo Anchorage and a fine bath for all the sleek naked bodies in the pool of the stream coming out from the lake. The crew decided to camp there, but I went on, wanting more miles and ready to go solo again.

A mile toward Fortuna Strait, my campsite instinct grabbed the paddle. I landed and checked, and it was a 10-point place. There was a high-tide island to protect the landing from rough seas, a flat area for the tent, a fire pit, two nearby streams, neither big enough for salmon runs and bears, remains of a cabin that said someone else had also found it good, sunrise and sunset views, green grass, flowers, a beachcombing strand with a glass ball on it, and the final touch of a small sign lettered: "No animals but birds, no bears."

On the overpopulated trails in the Lower 48, an obvious campsite is an intrusion on the wilderness we seek, but here, with so much wild country, it can be a clean and friendly thing.

The mushrooms were out now, this first week of August – now that I had sent the heavy mushroom book home because there had been so few in June and July. Most of these were *Russula*, most of them green or pink, one a bright carmine, and all of the day-old caps had been nibbled by the olive green-and-black three-inch-long banana slugs. A fresh one already had its slug curled possessively over it, munching contentedly.

The sack of dinners that I had prefabbed at home, packed into individual plastic bags for each meal, and mailed to Sitka still held a good variety. The corn fritters I chose for dinner were made from compressed freeze-dried corn and my own mix for batter, keeping to the yellow color scheme, of course, and in a day or two there would be cornmeal mush for breakfast. I set up the tent, read in bed, and blew the candle out at nine o'clock with the good feeling of a 12-mile day behind me and a home here. Tomorrow I would be out in the open sea on the west side of Chichagof Island. The nearest land beyond that would be Kodiak Island, 650 miles across the Gulf of Alaska.

Corn Fritters

Sift together:
½ cup flour
1 teaspoon baking powder
¼ teaspoon salt
2 teaspoons sugar

Work in:
1 teaspoon shortening
2 teaspoons dried egg powder
2 teaspoons powdered milk

Put mixture in ziplock bag. In camp, add water to make a stiff batter. Stir in ¾ cup of freeze-dried corn. Drop by teaspoonfuls into hot oil. Fry three or four at a time until brown. Serve with warm maple syrup.

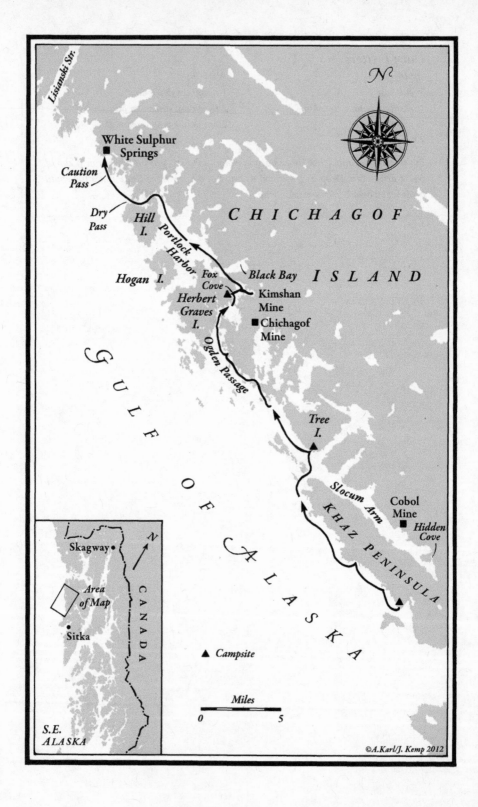

Open Seas and a Quest Fulfilled

For the first time, there was surf on the takeoff, and I had to time the wave sets, waiting for a lull. I paddled up the outside of the Khaz Peninsula, the "outside" that so many fishing crews had warned about, but they had been 10 miles out at sea and their memories included the storms of April and October, whereas I was paddling in August and hugging the coast. There were no headwinds, some surge, and need for a constant watch ahead, for white water breaking on rocks half a mile offshore. Shirtsleeves and bare hands most of the day.

This was a different kind of country. Halfway up the coast I stopped for lunch, cutting through rocky islets into an unnamed bay and over to the mouth of a stream. To the north was a spit of land with a ragged skyline of spruce and hemlock. The nine-foot high tide was just past, so I occasionally got up to float the boat out a bit farther and to loop the line over a lower rock. Along a shore of fist-size rocks was a strip of drying seaweed, evidence of the 11-foot tide that morning.

The sun was out, making a waving reflection of trees in the quiet blue water and turning the sea purslane to a vivid green mat. This plant, the most common one along the shores, has many names: the Latin *Honckenya peploides*, sea chickweed, sandwort, and just "beach greens." From southeastern Alaska to the Arctic it is eaten raw or cooked, and it's a good source of vitamins A and C. I was dipping it and goose tongue into a garlicky mayonnaise and sandwiching them between slabs of cheese, then sipping hot tea from my new Sitka thrift shop thermos bottle as I watched the scene. A few summers later, I found the greens far better when stir-fried with olive oil and garlic.

Landward of the northern cape was a quarter mile of flat, wooded land that local people called the potato patch, and behind it was the sudden lift of a 2,000-foot wrinkled half dome. East of it was the bare granite of Khaz Peak, and across the Khaz Peninsula, but out of sight and beyond the water of Slocum Arm, was the abandoned Cobol Mine, one of a dozen gold and silver mines on the west side of Chichagof Island that were operating in the 1930s. Not since Gut Bay had there been this alpine topography rising so steeply from the shore.

Always on this voyage there was a sense of space. I would stand on shore and slowly turn around, trying to absorb the limitless distance. So much of my life had been limited by the parameters of children, marriage, jobs, cities, neighbors, friends, expectations. Now there were none, and the sense of freedom was intense.

After only 10 miles of open ocean I came through in Piehle Passage and over to the first island, then to the second, both poor camping, then crossed east over to

Tree Island, a point with a stream, a high-tide islet, and a clear flat area in the dark woods with the remains of a log cabin. Had the builder panned for gold? Was there other evidence, such as a sluice box up the stream? Had he been here in the era of nearby Chichagof, Cobol, and Kimshan mines? The ends of the cabin logs were neatly squared, and the cabin was tucked back out of the wind. Perhaps he alternated between his miner's pick and his woodsman's axe, as I do all year between paddle, pen, spatula, and hammer.

Tree Island was an island only at high water; at low tide a rocky spit connected the tiny muffin of an islet with my campsite at the edge of the woods. On top of the island was a flat grassy spot just big enough for a tent or two sleeping bags. The stream on shore had a waterfall and a bathtub-size pool, but I wasn't that eager for an icy bath at bedtime.

To the south was Slocum Arm, the place that Tiger Olson, a famous old-timer who lived in Taku Harbor, near Juneau, called the prettiest place in Alaska. Someday, I would come back and explore it, all the way down to Hidden Cove. Someday, too, I would have a lower, sleeker, faster boat that averaged three knots instead of the two I was now getting. Maybe the power of the paddler makes the difference, Aud? Oh.

My nearby daytime sounds are easy to identify: the rusty-gate gargle of the eagle, the single oboe note of the varied thrush, the eerie warble of the loon. It's the unknown night sounds that can terrify, and before I crawl into the sleeping bag I listen for what I'm likely to hear in the dark. Are those spruce needles, scratching like claws against the tent? Is that heavy thump a drift log shifting in the falling tide? On later voyages, back in the narrow shipping lanes of the Inside Passage from Skagway into British Columbia, I would waken to the sound of crashing waves cast from a passing cruise ship, and I'd leap out to see if my boat were really tied high enough. Here on the outside of all the islands, no ships pass, only a few fishing boats, and the sense of space and solitude is intense day and night.

In the morning, breakfast, as usual, was oatmeal, eaten as I sat on a log. It's oatmeal that stays with me, gives the all-day stamina. There's a noticeable difference between that and any other breakfast. Sure and 'tis your Scottish imagination. Sure and 'tis the lack of me oats. You're confusing your Scottish and Irish dialects, Aud. I know. Got to paddle both places and straighten out my language. After every breakfast, as I scrape the pot, I think of why the Scots are so strong and courageous. I canna remember the origin of the story, but it's been with me for years, and my own bairns were served the story along with the oats:

> *"Once upon a time, before china bowls were brought to Europe, the heavy timbered tables in Scotland had bowls carved down into the wood at each place. The children were always hungry, so they ate every bit of oatmeal each morning. Over the years, the steady scraping of their spoons slowly carved the bowls deeper, so that each generation was served a bit more*

oatmeal than had filled the bowls of their fathers. And that's why the Scots are so brawny and brave."

My children laughed, flexed their muscles, and scraped their bowls.

The *Miss Susan*, a gill-netter, came in close, spotting for fish, I guessed. I waved, but they were busy. I like at least to let them know that the yellow boat is not just debris washed up here on a log. A plane was lost two weeks ago, and search planes have been out. The fishing boats must also be reporting any possible wreckage by radio.

I'd slept deeply that night, too deeply for safety perhaps, or maybe it's better that way. We all have become too psyched for bears. When I see none, no scat, no claw marks on the trees, no tracks, no trails except of mink and deer, no salmon jumping or packed ready to run up a stream, then I figure I'm reasonably safe. Sometimes, then, I just pack my ears with cotton so as not to wake to every twig snapping. I need to sleep.

The fondue was excellent last night: Swiss cheese, garlic, the wine from a foil bag, and crusty rolls from the Shee Atika hotel's buffet in Sitka. You put them in your pocket? I did.

I sat there planning a cabin just eight feet square to put on top of Tree Island: a 360-degree view. Two sheets of plywood for the floor, another for a deck, a slanting shed roof so as to have room for a bunk up under the high side over the door. You'd be better off tucking your cabin back in the woods out of the wind, Aud. A winter storm would pick it up and blow the scattered pieces all the way down Slocum Arm. That would be only fair, as most of the lumber would have been flotsam culled from Alaska's beaches, a natural step after the years I've been wearing salvage-colored glasses and dialing the mind to "freesam" on the highways and freeways.

Dream cabins even have sunshine coming through an east window in the morning. Then there's Millay:

> *"... build a little shanty on the sand*
> *In such a way that the extremest band*
> *Of brittle seaweed will escape my door*
> *But by a yard or two ..."*

A bit more than a yard for winter storms. Are you going to be here in the winter, lady? Good question. Winter cabins should be sturdier, insulated, and not quite so isolated: perhaps only five miles from town if I'm going to be alone and have to paddle in for supplies.

Why is it that when you live in that most marvelous of all climes, Hawai'i, you keep wanting to be here in this rainy, cold, windy country? Because it isn't overrun with people. A high desert, too, would have this feeling of space and this sense of a natural order in which I daily make my own small niche.

The kayak and I, a single entity after all these weeks, moved on. It was as if we had become some mythical creature, not a centaur, half man, half horse, or a mermaid, half woman, half fish, but a new creature, half human, half boat. A kaymaid, a sheyak, a boatress, a Tuplass – as in Tupperware-like plastic boats, but "to tup"? No way. In Hawai'i I would be a kaimaid, as *kai* means "the sea." The possibilities kept the new critter occupied for miles.

I passed Double Cove, with its portage to Sister Lake marked on the chart, then paddled against the tides of Smooth Channel, which were moving east into Klag Bay, where the old Chichagof mine was being reopened. I moved west, out into Ogden Passage and into the small cove marked Indian Village, but only moss-covered planks remained. Two miles to the left on a small island was a visible cabin, mentioned in Margaret Piggott's *Discover Southeast Alaska with Pack and Paddle*. She said it had been vandalized, but her standards may be higher than mine. Everything is relative. An intact roof and three walls of a chicken coop are a luxury when it's cold and raining. Ahead was Frog Rock, so obviously a frog that I laughed and paddled over to blow him a kiss, but a kaymaid is not a princess, and he remained enchanted as a frog, patiently waiting.

In Fox Cove was an old float cabin of three rooms with a rusty woodstove from the foundry in Lunenberg, Nova Scotia, that looked as if it belonged on a square-rigger. Since it had an oven, dinner was a casserole of cheesy sour-cream pasta, a mango-apple cobbler, and the last of a Tjesseling Petite Sirah. In the morning it was yellow, crispy cornmeal mush fried in the cabin's big skillet. I ranged the shore for driftwood to replace what I had used, bringing it back in the boat and cutting it up with my folding bucksaw.

In the afternoon I paddled over to Kimshan Cove. There were remains of several houses, one with an intact fireplace. The bunkhouse was in good condition, evidently maintained by present mining claims. Now that the price of gold is high, the old mines are being reclaimed and checked to see if they're worth working again. It was $30 an ounce back in the 1930s. Now it is more than $1,800 an ounce, but the cost of equipment and labor is also at least 10 times greater. The bunkhouse visitors' log for the past four years showed kayakers, yacht people, and fishing-boat crews.

Outside on the mud flats, without digging, I picked up a dozen big cockles. Meatier than clams, bigger than mussels, these heart cockles can be cooked in many ways. Euell Gibbons, whose *Beachcomber's Handbook* is the best book on Hawai'i food gathering, has pages on clams and cockles in *Stalking the Blue-Eyed Scallop*. I was also searching for giant bull kelp, to make pickles and even to experiment with candied kelp – an unlikely product, but so is cactus candy, and the Mexicans do that well. The Chinese make squash candy. I could try kelp.

I paddled back to Fox Cove and finally left at 4:00 pm, planning to get in about four hours' paddling and then camp somewhere. Out through Surveyor Passage I had a tailwind and an ebbing tide, then the wind shifted 90 degrees and pushed me across Portlock Harbor. A Klepper kayak fought upwind through the rain toward me. I hailed it, thinking it was some of my Harvard crew, but it was part of a group led by

Ken Leghorn of Alaska Discovery Inc, based in Juneau and heading back to their own tour group in Black Bay. The Klepper did look very efficient, but it weighs 75 pounds, and I could not have carried it alone above high tide every night.

It was great to find that I was not the only one mad enough to paddle in this weather, but of course if you wait for sunny days to paddle in southeastern Alaska, you might be able to travel 20 miles a month. We wished each other dry days and tailwinds, and said good-bye.

The rain was increasing. I paddled over to the isthmus above Dry Pass and walked through to take a look at the ocean beyond. It was only three more miles to the cabin at White Sulphur Springs, and the seas looked possible, so I walked back to the boat and ran through the pass at five knots on an outgoing tide. Out into the open sea with the wind picking up from the southeast and a swell coming in from the west: big and sloppy, but possible. It was getting dark, and it was hard to steer and read the chart at the same time to compare it with the headlands. There was a narrow sheltered pass over to the right somewhere, but I headed for Caution Pass, which I could see ahead. I sang as I paddled, "My paddle's keen and bright, flashing like silver. Swift as the wild goose flight. Dip, dip, and swing."

Laughing at my own bravado, because I was scared.

"Boat, you did fine on that last sloppy white wave, slewing a bit, but all right."

Talk out loud, pretend you're two people, someone to help you when you capsize. Remember Clarence Strait, and delicately balance to finesse each peaking wave.

Once into Caution Pass, the seas calmed. I paddled out of the pass into Bertha Bay and on toward shore. Outlines of buildings ahead, then, "Damn, a light." People there. I had hoped they wouldn't come in this weather. My reservation for the cabin was not until tomorrow. Into shore, at low tide, I looped the boat line on barnacled rocks. I carried a load over seaweed, then rounded boulders, then drift logs. Wet and cold, I knocked at the cabin door. Four teenagers. I asked about a flat area for camping and said I had canoed in from Ketchikan. They didn't know of anyplace. Period. I walked away.

"It isn't their fault if you're dumb enough to arrive in the rain at 11:00 pm, Aud," sneered the critic.

"You're right," said the paddler.

I went back and hauled another load, then brought up the boat. There was a separate bathhouse cabin 50 feet west, and the water flowing out beneath it was warm. A third load of gear, then looked into the bath. Ahhh yes, later. The tarp and tent went up in record time on a small semiflat area. I put the sleeping bag and mattress inside, plus a bit of cheese and wine, made sure the boat was well tied and that the bags of gear were under it out of the rain, then went into the bath with candle and towel.

The pool was eight feet wide, with boulders on the sides and a cement dam at the end. Shoji sliding doors opened to the view or closed off the chill ocean air. I scrubbed and rinsed on the deck, then eased in, finally touching bottom five feet deep, all the

while whimpering orgasmic moans and gasps of delight. I soaked and floated until the warmth permeated bone deep, then dried and pulled on the old cashmere and wool underwear, the foul-weather gear over it, and went blissfully off to a dry bed in a rainy world.

I slept until nine o'clock, then walked the trail east to Mirror Harbor, where a big power yacht was anchored. En route back I found a trail to a small lake, but not until the next day did I find the best campsite and landing beach, about 100 yards west of the cabin, along a trail that also crossed a cold-water stream.

I went back to the cabin. It was noon and the place was mine. The kids were gone and had left a nice note. I spent the first hour cleaning up and the next two moving in — to the sound of rock music, as they came back with a radio, three dogs, and parents, to use the yard, the bath, the fire pit, and the small outside pool. When they left, all that remained were cigarette and roach butts, dog shit, cans, shampoo bottles, soap scum on the pool, an empty firewood shed, and four names carved deep on the cedar walls of the bathhouse: Mike, Barb, Karen, and Diane.

Nice kids, no doubt, just average American folks. No doubt I was getting old and crotchety. At least papa had picked up the sack of trash I'd collected and carried it off to his boat.

I skimmed the pool water, scrubbed and rinsed on deck until I was squeaky clean, then slid in to soak in the 106-degree water. Such a joy. When I walked out there were two people waiting. Two sentences and we were communicating. They bathed, then came in for tea. Lee and Holly were from Sitka, and had been long-line fishing for several years.

"It's time to quit and go on to something else," Lee said.

We talked of vocational choices. It seemed a long time since I'd used my profession. Lee wanted a technical field; Holly liked languages, especially Japanese. We went through some exercises I had used in group counseling sessions. One question was the one I had asked myself and answered with this voyage.

"If you had a year to do anything you wanted, and had all the money you needed, and could come back to where you are now, what would you do?

Most people had been living on expediency: what needed to be done that hour, that day. They'd never asked the big question. When they had the answer, my next question was, "Why aren't you doing it?"

Then came the obvious answers. "I don't have the money. I do have kids, a family, a job, a mortgage."

"When can you do it? Can you do part of it? How can you plan toward it?"

We all need to ask those questions every five years, then act on the answers. You get plenty of advice on planning your whole life, but five years is long enough. After age 50 you can narrow it down to a two-year plan. Beyond 60, it's a one-year plan. Beyond that?

I made a pot of chicken Tetrazzini and learned more about fishing in Alaska.

"Going downhill," said Lee – the same answer I'd heard from all the crews I'd talked with.

Lee and Holly left in the rain for the mile walk to the harbor and the half-mile row in a skiff to their boat. I admired them both and wished them well. What a good antidote. I bathed again, for pure sensuous pleasure, and slept on four inches of foam pad some other good person had brought.

The stove was a new airtight type, a Reginald 100, that kept a stump burning all afternoon and evening. The cabin was the standard 12 by 14 cedar Pan-Abode and needed only one thing, to be placed 100 yards away from the hot spring, so that each could have privacy from the other. It must be wonderful here in winter, with snow and solitude, and the steaming pool inside the bathhouse.

All day a south wind blew, with rain and rough seas out in the bay. I made kelp pickles, a mix of kelp rings, sugar, and vinegar simmered until tender, then canned them in six jars I'd collected from beaches along the way. I had planned on making jam and had a sugar supply, but the berries were all gone. I forgot to try the candied kelp. As long as the wind held from the south, I'd take the rough seas and rain in preference to a headwind when I paddled up the long length of Lisianski Strait and across Icy Strait to Glacier Bay.

I went out to the area of drift logs on the shore, looking for dimensional lumber or plywood to repair the cabin's wood box. Ninety-eight percent of driftwood is logs. They have their own beauty; shades of blond and gray, curved and hollowed and sleeked like a human body – or perhaps we're like them – aged and smoothed by years of tumbling in the seas and on the rocks.

Then the Harvard paddlers arrived. That made seven of us in the small cabin, drying gear, bathing, exchanging books. I read their copy of John Dowd's *Sea Kayaking* and learned about canoeist's arm, "a creeping numbness which begins in the fingers, and sometimes works its way up the hand, wrist, and arm to the shoulder." My symptoms precisely, and with adequate cause. Along with all the technical information in the book, the tough gentle character of the author came through. One hundred–mile open sea crossings in a kayak in 50-knot winds: My deep respect to John and Beatrice Dowd.

Next morning the crew left, and I packed up also. I was down to less gear now, less food, more room for the jars of pickles, which I would mail home from Elfin Cove. I was hating the thought of departure. At last the hot springs quest had come true, and if the cabins seemed too civilized, I could wait for an unpeopled moment, or for winter, and sit in the shallow warm pool just at the edge of woods and beach, and feel it the way it had been 100, or 1,000, years ago, with only the sky for a ceiling.

Turkey or Chicken Tetrazzini

4 large dried shiitake mushrooms, or an equivalent
1 cup dry pasta
½ to 1 cup dry white wine.
2 packets dried mushroom or chicken soup
1 5-oz. can turkey or chicken chunks

Soak mushrooms in ½ cup water for five minutes. Save water. Cook pasta in 2 cups boiling water. When tender, drain. Add mushrooms and soaking water and wine. Stir in soup powder and chicken. Bring to a boil. Adjust liquid amount (I like it slurpy). You can add cheese or TVP (textured vegetable protein), or chopped fresh onion or onion flakes, or use shucked mussels instead of chicken. Serve over pasta.

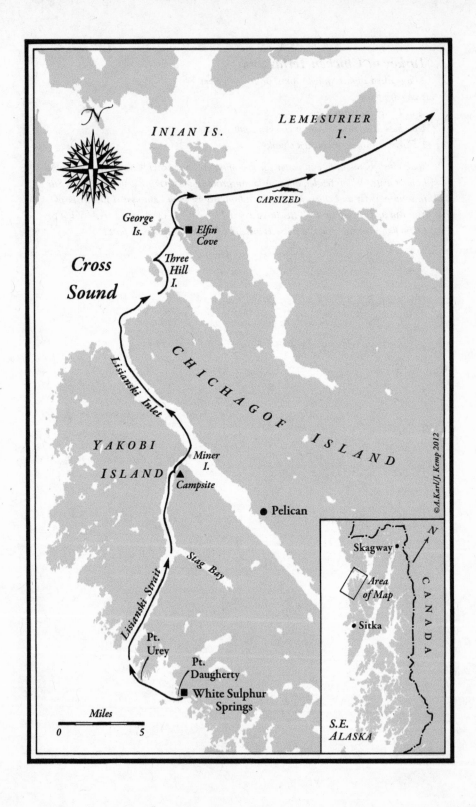

N

INIAN IS.

LEMESURIER
I.

CAPSIZED

George
Is.

■ Elfin
Cove

Cross
Sound

Three
Hill
I.

Lisianski Inlet

C H I C H A G O F

I S L A N D

YAKOBI

ISLAND

Miner
I.

▲
Campsite

● Pelican

©A.Karl/J.Kemp 2012

Lisianski Strait

Stag Bay

Pt.
Urey

Pt.
Daugherty

■ White Sulphur
Springs

Miles

0   5

N

Skagway ●

Area
of Map

C A N A D A

● Sitka

S.E.
ALASKA

CAPSIZE AND GLACIER BAY

The morning body had the usual stiffness for the first half hour's paddling, but soon warmed up. I should have spent two minutes stretching. Two months ago, my pace had been 20 strokes a minute. Now it was 30.

Out and around the first point, then past Point Dougherty with big swells from the south; Hawai'i was out there, too, in a straight line 2,000 miles away. A bit of shelter in the lee of the Porcupine Islands, then swells again. Once past the rocks ahead I would be halfway to Point Urey. It was hard to maneuver because of the thick kelp. For the first time, I was certain I was seeing sea otters, not seals, as feet showed, not fins, when they humped over to dive. The sun had been shining all morning, and a strange event was happening: Sweat was dripping off my nose as I paddled through the kelp, the first sweat since Hawai'i.

On into the strait named for the Neva's captain, Urey Lisianski, who also gave names to many of the places near the coast in Alaska. I had a tailwind, an incoming tide, and clear views of the mountains. Far ahead was the snowcapped Fairweather Range with its 15,000-foot peaks.

Salmon had been jumping, and I rigged the fishing gear to troll a line. In three minutes a fish struck hard. Since hooks, fish spines, and inflatable boats are not an advisable mix, I braced the pole between thigh and boat, looked for the nearest beach, and paddled to shore. One hand held the jerking pole; the other paddled, then looped the lifeline to a rock. I played the fish toward the shore while using my free hand to pull the camera off my neck, screw it to the tripod, and set the self-timer to record shots of the action. That eight-pound fighting coho, finally landed and bagged, was going to provide several lunches and dinners.

The wind and tide stayed my way for another two hours, then both slowed. I kept watching the kelp. Rooted to the bottom, the long stems reached up to the surface, buoyed by a bulbous air sac; the long fronds streamed in the direction of the currents, flowing like Rapunzel's golden hair.

Just short of the charted light at the north end of the strait was a campsite. A stream, plenty of wood, and the shortest haul in a month. There was a strange formation of wispy torn clouds to the west. I built a fire on layers of dry plywood and scrap metal, as a wet moss base doesn't work, and after Devils Elbow cabin I knew now about organic soil that burned. I seldom build a campfire; it insulates me from the night and the natural world and takes away my night vision, but occasionally I do want the fire warmth that humans have been building for half a million years. I also needed to smoke some salmon. Earlier I had spotted a five-gallon can on shore and brought it along. One end was gone. Perfect. I punched holes in both sides of the can and wired in one side of my grate. Holding the grate in place with one knee, I placed the marinated chunks of salmon, then wired the other side. The fire was down to coals, and I added sticks of half-green alder, placed the can on top, and chinked around the base with wet earth.

Off to bed, with the tent across the stream from the smoke oven. It didn't feel like bear country, and there was no evidence of any. Nineteen easy miles today.

The red light marking the mid-strait island had been flashing at five-second intervals all night, but at dawn it was obscured by solid fog. So that's what those clouds meant. The other side of the strait was invisible, half a mile away. Breakfast, then checked the smoke oven. The salmon was perfect, a soft-smoked product that would keep only for a week or so, just long enough to eat it all.

I left in the fog on a magnetic north course, the compass between my knees. A mountain ridge showed softly ahead, and a sun dog, an ellipse of light like a rainbow, lay over the water to the left. I passed Miner Island, where the tides meet and change. The tide was going out now, down Lisianski Inlet, but a northwest wind came up. I crossed the inlet and decided to have lunch and wait out the wind. The sun came out, and so did many fishing boats. There was a clear view all the way southeast up the inlet to the village of Pelican, an unlikely name for a town here, as there are no pelicans in Alaska.

Down the inlet I paddled, around the white water at the base of the rock steles of Column Point, and out into the rolling swells of Cross Sound. Far out to the northwest, beyond Cape Spencer, was the open sea route to Lituya Bay, where an earthquake and a gigantic landslide on July 9, 1958, had caused a 50-foot displacement wave to rise up the spur ridge across the bay, stripping it of trees to a height of 1,720 feet. Three boats were in the bay at the time, and two miraculously survived. Four years later, I would hear the story of the wave and of one of those boats, the *Edrie*, from its competent skipper, Howard Ulrich, who had been on that boat with his six-year-old son and who now was captain, cook, and mate of the Forest Service boat *Sitka Ranger*. The Lituya Bay story is also well told in the book *Land of the Ocean Mists*, by Francis Caldwell and Robert DeArmond, and also in *Wildest Alaska*, by Philip L. Fradkin.

Beyond Lituya was the long route to Yakutat, with rows of breaking surf, making it impossible to land and launch my boat. That would be the outside route to the northwestern point of the Alaskan Panhandle. I was going the inside route to the northeastern point, Skagway.

I turned right – "Starboard, you lubber," I corrected myself – heading for the Elfin Cove settlement. Ahead was a rock island covered with gulls. As I sat watching, a 15-foot whale with a hooked dorsal fin rolled by for a quick glimpse of this yellow animal. It looked like the minke whale on my sheet of silhouette identifications. I paddled on to Three Hill Island, with its clear water and eroded columns.

The crew of a powerboat, the *Hunky Dory*, asked if I needed help.

"No, I'm fine. Just taking photos."

Ten minutes later, a troller with poles spread at a 45-degree angle and lines running back from the gurdies, the power winches, asked if I wanted a tow. These Elfin Cove people were a rare breed!

"No, thanks very much."

I should have accepted. He was the first fisherman to invite me. I couldn't learn about Alaska-style fishing and how it differed from the Southern California albacore fishing I had done for those three years long ago unless I were aboard. But towing is a risky business: hooks, lines, cables, the curling waves of the wake, all could tear and dump my rig. Better to stay solo at my own slow pace.

I was tiring now, knowing I was overdoing it, but paddled slowly across the three miles and into the narrow entrance of the cove. Civilization again, the first town since Sitka, but the year-round population of about 40 wasn't city size.

At the dock I tied up between skiffs and walked up the ramp. Tony, the efficient cook at the Elf Inn, made a $6.50 hamburger that was worth the price. I laughed to realize that even after my exotic haute-cuisine meals, I still went straight for a hamburger when I came into town.

A pair of booted fisherman on the next swivel stools asked, "You come off a boat?"

I nodded and pointed an elbow toward the small yellow craft.

"Where's your big boat?"

"That's it."

"Were you the one out in Cross Sound?"

Mouth full, I nodded.

"Where'd you come from?"

I mumbled, "Ketchikan."

"In that?!"

Nod.

"Alone?"

"Yes."

After they had commented on insane women, I got good advice about the next day's crossing of Icy Strait.

A buyer barge was at the end of the floating dock with a supply store for the fishing boats. While buying my own supplies I had my first look at a king salmon, a very impressive animal, and it only confirmed my decision that I would limit my own fishing to the smaller species and that I'd keep my knife handy to cut loose anything that felt like this size.

Next morning I mailed off the kelp pickles, then wandered up to meet Augusta and Roy Clemens, whom I'd heard about back at Point Baker. They were another of

the old-time capable Alaskan couples scattered throughout the southeast in the small settlements or in isolated nooks. The Elfin Cove street was a boardwalk clinging to the cliffside, maintained by the highway division of the State of Alaska. I walked along the planked lane past old wooden houses. The boardwalk became a trail; the houses perched on the slope. There were spruce needles underfoot, ferns and berries along the way in the dim light under the trees. Augusta was accustomed to visitors; she continued cutting halibut and salmon into three-inch squares to smoke over alderwood. Kelp pickles, pies, and cookies were on the table, and the scent of freshly baked bread came from the ovens. I had samples of warm raspberry jam, good coffee, and took pages of notes for feeding myself even better.

My six kayaking friends arrived in Elfin Cove and arranged a ride for themselves on the *Kris*, a fishing boat, across the treacherous South Inian Pass and Icy Strait to Glacier Bay. I paddled off solo in the early afternoon to catch the incoming tide through the Pass, where the outgoing current can reach nine knots. I went through at low slack with an imperceptible current, and headed toward Lemesurier Island to camp. A few miles later, the *Kris* with its crew plus the kayakers caught up.

I was holding a line from their boat, talking to the group, deciding whether to paddle or ride or tow for a bit. The skipper picked up speed only slightly, and I slacked off on the line to fall back into a side tow. It was just enough to let their heavy boat's bow wave come back between my light craft and theirs, enough to lift my port side and roll me neatly and precisely upside down.

I came to the surface instantly, tethered to my boat by the lifeline over my shoulder. The water was numbing; Icy Strait it was, indeed. The boots didn't pull me down, but they were full of water and sliding down, about to come off and sink. The bags of gear were still under the boat. I was on the same side as my lifeline. I needed to swim around to the other side, leading the line up and across the bottom of the boat so as to pull the line taut and flip the boat upright. I swam to the end of the boat, keeping my knees bent tightly to hold the boots on, thinking I could flip it from the stern, but I couldn't get enough leverage. Hell, just wait.

The fishing boat circled and was back to me in two minutes, the kayakers standing along the side, aghast. I handed up the boots, then the bags, paddle, and the line to my boat, and then climbed up, and we pulled the boat over the side to the deck. Judy fired up the cabin's oil stove, and I went below to strip and rub dry, shivering violently. I unpacked my clothes bag, put on the dry wool underwear, a sweater, wool pants, dry socks, and dry shoes. Nothing was lost, not even the wool cap, only a bit of pride.

It was a good lesson. I needed to rig a clip loop for the boots and hang it from the boat. Alone, I'd need to get the gear out from under the boat, or flip the boat up and off the gear to right it. I needed to hold the paddle line and lead it, too, over the boat to assist in flipping it. These inflatables had three major safety advantages over fiberglass boats. They rested on their buoyant sides when capsized, draining out all the water. When flipped upright, no water remained inside. Second, they were far easier to climb back into than most rigid boats, with their narrow cockpits and rolling hulls, where you always felt you needed knees that bent the other way. Third, these boats had their own buoyancy. You didn't have to take up cargo space with air bags, or use an alternate system of weighty bulkheads, which often seemed to twist and leak through their walls or through their hatches.

The decision to paddle or to ride the remaining 18 miles past Lemesurier Island and on to Glacier Bay had been made by my own error. I kept watching the rough seas of Icy Strait, and was glad to be aboard.

"When you get to Skagway you can't count this as mileage paddled, Aud. For sure not."

I kept reliving the capsize in my mind. All the literature said you could live for 30 to 45 minutes in 40-degree water, depending on your body fat, wool clothing, and ability to hunch into a fetal position so as not to lose heat from armpits and groin. But it might be only 10 minutes until I was so numb that my body could not respond to my mind's commands. I had often climbed back into the boat in Hawai'i, but there I was wearing fins and bikini, so that I could roll out and swim along, towing the boat while viewing the underwater scene. The idea then was also to use some leg muscles as a change from arm-and-shoulder paddling stress.

I had better practice capsizing while wearing boots, pile pants, shirt, foul-weather bib pants and jacket, gloves, and a cap, with all the bags of gear in the boat. I had to get the boat upright, then get into it. To slide into the boat I had to first kick my legs up parallel to the surface, reach across and push down on the far side while I slid in across the near side. Mental rehearsals were fine – I was gyrating in body English as I thought through the steps – but the brain-muscle circuits had to be trained also. Practice it a dozen times, in 20-knot winds, with all gear and cold-water clothing, until you don't have to think, just act.

At the dock of Bartlett Cove in Glacier Bay National Park, I thanked the boat skippers, contributed for fuel, then offloaded my gear and paddled down to the parklike campground. I walked back carrying a soggy load of clothes for the lodge's washer and dryer, then back again to set up camp, putting most of my food into the log cache, fortified against bears. Tent and tarp up, I walked the winding trail on a different route to the lodge, noting wild strawberries near the beach.

Away from shore it became a fairy-tale forest. Less than 200 years before, the land had emerged from under the retreating glaciers. When Captain George Vancouver sailed through Icy Strait in 1794, still searching for a Northwest Passage to connect with the Atlantic Ocean, there was not even a bay to be seen; the five-mile-wide mouth of Glacier Bay was covered with ice. Then, rapidly for glaciers, the ice had retreated. First lichens appeared on the bare rocks, then other plants. *Dryas* was one of the pioneers, a delicate, puffy-seeded plant, blowing in the wind, blowing its seeds across the rocks and into the tiny pockets of newly formed silt and dried lichen. Alder sprouts contributed nitrogen to the land to nourish other plants. Finally, the spruces and hemlocks grew up to top the alder, and it disappeared, except in thickets along the shore.

I was walking though a young forest. None of the trees had matured enough to shed old branches or to drop of old age in the usual jumble of fallen giants. You could walk in this forest, softly stepping on the moss to kneel down and examine a mushroom. And now, at last, another of my voyage's themes, the quest for edible fungi along the route, was coming to pass.

By the end of the first day at the campground, out on a beach log near the tent, were a dozen jars, cups, and cans, each covering a mushroom cap which was slowly dropping its spore print onto a sheet of paper in individualized patterns, with the colors to help in the identification. Soon I had six firmly named and rated as edible, good, or choice selections for dinner. Some were old friends, some new. One of the most easily identified and delicious was *Dentinum repandum,* with toothlike nodules instead of gills. Another was a vivid purple one, shaped like coral, but purple food seemed very strange. Still, bears made purple piles from blueberries ...

No single mushroom reference book was adequate, and I used the park library to cross check, meeting there another new friend, Doris Howe, volunteer librarian and wife of the former park superintendent, Robert Howe.

Glacier Bay was a national park that lived up to all the writers' superlatives. No way could you swing by the place while driving on a blurry vacation to include seven parks in six states in five days. You went to Glacier Bay on purpose, by plane and bus, by cruise ship, or by private boat. There were kayaks to rent within the park; a few people, like my friends, brought their own, but there probably weren't more than 30 kayaks that year paddling into Glacier Bay Park from another area.

Meanwhile, the daily film showings, nature walks, and pamphlets from the desk in the lodge were answering the questions I'd been storing up for two months. The naturalists were knowledgeable, helpful, and delighted with their jobs.

To see the glaciers, still melting in retreat, I would need to go up one of the arms of the bay. It would be 60 miles, six to eight days of bare cold country; there were as yet no forests up the bay. I mashed down the Scottish soul, bought a ticket for the daily cruise ship, and rose at six the next morning and dressed in all the layers of clothes I owned. We cruised up past the Beardslee Islands, past Strawberry Island, emerging from forested land into a barren country with its own stark beauty, like the lava fields of Hawai'i. Mike Rivers, our onboard ranger-naturalist, explained what we were seeing. Then we moved in close to the Marble Islands. Birds! Pigeon guillemots, cormorants, common murres, murrelets, black oystercatchers, and who could help being delighted by the real thing from the poem:

> "There once was a puffin shaped just like a muffin
> Who lived on an island in the deep blue sea."

If you aren't a bird-watcher when you come to Glacier Bay, you become one. Sea creatures had always seemed more enchanting than birds, but here the birds were sea animals. A sea otter had been my ideal reincarnation form, or perhaps a selchie, the mystical half human, half seal of the Outer Hebrides, but after Alaska that changed. Next time around I would be a loon or merganser, or a pigeon guillemot. They can all swim a long distance under water and fly.

Throughout the whole voyage I had been watching guillemots. When I came within 50 feet they would suddenly decide it was too close, paddle rapidly away, and then flap their wings, trying to get airborne. The red feet would keep paddling as they rose, beating the water in a frantic toe dance, like the hippopotamus en pointe in Disney's classic film *Fantasia*.

The endearing marbled murrelet, with its single peep like a baby chick, was smaller, and usually dove to escape, but sometimes it flew off, the stubby little body hitting the water several times before it was aloft, like a child's flat stone skipping on a pond. Now there is a whole book about the marbled murrelet, *Rare Bird*, by Maria Mudd-Ruth.

At Muir Point we dropped off 12 teenagers with six kayaks, then dropped and picked up more at Riggs Glacier. The cost of a drop-off was the same as a tour, $27. At Riggs, the captain turned off the engine, and we floated there in the silence, listening to the voice of the glacier, snapping and cracking and sometimes calving off a wall of ice, the birth of an iceberg. Because of its crystalline structure, the glacial ice absorbs all colors except blue, which it reflects. The passengers stood quietly on deck, rapt, awed. Near me a woman breathed, "Thank you, Lord."

That was what we had come so far to see and feel. The faces were the same as those watching an eruption of lava in Volcano National Park in Hawai'i. This wasn't just a quiet piece of scenery. It was a living, breathing, birthing part of the earth.

In my tent that night I reread Dave Bohn's *Glacier Bay: the Land and the Silence*. I envied him. The years that went into it, and the book that came out of the years, were more than enough to fulfill a lifetime: It doesn't matter what he did before or after. A book like that justifies an author's place on earth for 90 years.

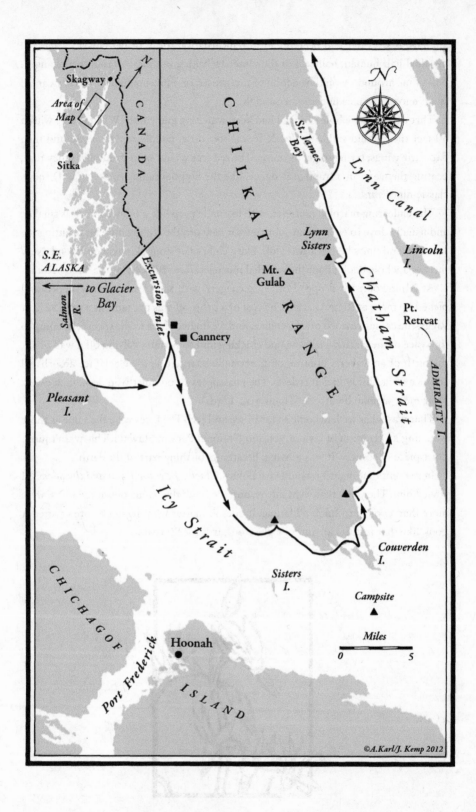

WOLF AT BREAKFAST

Two days later and 10 miles east, I launched into the turbid Salmon River of the Gustavus glacial plain. Doris Howe watched, sitting quietly on the bank as I paddled down between the grass and mud shores toward the sea. The wind was rising with a steady light rain, my foul-weather jacket and pants were leaking, and that wind was from the southeast, its usual direction when I was heading southeast. What a beginning for the final week!

I tried lining the boat, walking on shore and towing it, but even a slow paddle was faster. There were mud flats ahead, so I crossed to Pleasant Island, named by John Muir and the missionary Hall Young in 1879. Lunch was a granola bar and a new batch of smoked salmon from Ann and Jim Mackovyak of Gustavus, another pioneer couple with the independent lifestyle that Alaskans treasure. After a few miles along the lee shore of the island, I headed out again into Icy Strait and east to the long peninsula, looking now for campsites, but all were rocky and none was flat.

Excursion Inlet ahead was supposed to have a good store. What else was up there, and why hadn't I researched it? Through the rain I paddled toward the lights, which slowly enlarged into a cold storage plant with people up on the pier busily loading fish. Farther on was a small-boat dock; there I unpacked the bags and lifted the boat onto the float, as the surge was too strong to leave it bouncing and rubbing the dock.

Don McLean, the night watchman, kindly gave me use of a dormitory that was being built for the cold storage and cannery workers. His cheese omelet at breakfast demonstrated his wintertime profession of cook. My voyage from Ketchikan didn't mean much to him, nor the destination of Skagway, as he'd flown to Alaska from Seattle and didn't know the distances, but he understood that I'd been traveling since June and thought I'd gone about 700 miles so far.

At the store I bought a few supplies and loaded up. It was easy paddling, with the wind down from yesterday and a thin sun through the drizzle. This was a well-known fishing ground called the Home Shore, and many boats were out, the small hand trollers designated by H.T. lettered on the side. They had a cheaper license, fewer regulations, and the winches were cranked by hand, not power. Maybe my boat ought finally to be christened, if not *Kaymaid* or *Selchie*, then perhaps the *H.T. Puffer*.

The route was north, but I had to go south first, down to the end of the peninsula, then east to Lynn Canal. Out three miles to the right was the Sisters Island light. Hour by hour I moved around the curve, moving that light toward my stern. Already it was time to find a camp; the days were getting shorter. The next landing beach had a Forest

Service sign, "Bald Eagle Nest Tree," but neither eagles nor nest were aloft. Fine, I wasn't about to camp under either one. A cabin had been here long before, with old boards and a rusty washbasin the only remnants.

Dinner was going to be a celebration. Once around the tip of the peninsula tomorrow, I'd be in Lynn Canal, the final waterway to the final goal of Skagway. No more resupplies. This was it, the last lap.

I pulled out the bag of ingredients for beef hekka, mailed from Hawai'i by my cosmopolitan friend Trixie. The strings of dried gourd were six feet long, but I soaked them, and then, in an improbable maneuver, tied them in a series of overhand knots and cut between them. The freeze-dried pieces of tofu had the flavor and consistency of small sponges, so I scattered them for the squirrels, but ate the good stewed gourd, sauce, and shiitake mushrooms.

Why such an emphasis on food throughout this trip? There were few physical pleasures – rarely any clean clothes, seldom any warmth of sun, firelight, or a bath, and no time to build any warm human communication. Food was pleasurable to the taste, provided sheer warmth in the belly, and had the satisfaction of a creative art form, the craft of cuisine. There was also the half-spoof goal of the gourmet kitchen, and the real need of the body for fuel to power the 48,000 pounds of water moved in paddling each day.

I could have foraged more. David J. Cooper, in his book *Brooks Range Passage*, describes gathering much of his food from plants as he walked the 120 miles to the Arrigetch Peaks. But only a limited variety of plants grew on shore here, and I needed the time for traveling, not foraging. Sometimes during the long hours of steady paddling I envisioned a different kind of trip. No gadgets or plastic bagged meals. My three-pound tent was adequate to keep bugs out, but the Gore-Tex fabric, once clogged with salt air, no longer shed water, and I had to rig the tarp over it each night. The open tarp keeps the rain off, but the air that blows under is so heavy with water and salt that nothing stays dry unless I leave it bagged. I would design a new tent myself, large enough to stand in, with walls. I think I could design and build a tiny portable woodstove also, as I had a fireplace for the VW bus in Europe years ago. Take fishing gear, a Bic lighter not matches, an old pot, a saw, coffee, a skillet and grate, and a kayak of longer, lower proportions.

I would have no schedules, avoid towns and people. Use more outside routes; take one island, Baranof or Kuiu, and go around it, into every bay. Listen and look and smell until I forgot the body and felt like just another animal, wary but capable of living in this country, the senses alert, the animal instincts reborn.

Doing what you want to do isn't a question of can you or can't you, yes or no, but deciding what your ultimate desire and capability is and then figuring out the steps to accomplishment. It's "I'm going to. Now how? What gear will I need? What skills will I need? What will it cost? When will it happen? When I succeed, what next?"

Coming back to the present, I used the rusty washbasin as a base for a wood fire and warmed the clammy sleeping bag, while heating hot sake. Not for me a thimble-size sake cup. The quarter-cup of rice wine could be heated directly over the flame in my two-cup enameled mug, which was large enough to cover my nose while I sipped, sending the pungent hot fumes up my nostrils while the hot wine went down my throat: double-duty value.

September 1. More mushrooms had popped up overnight from the autumn season and the rain. In the usual two hours I was under way. At home, where I know precisely where everything is, I can lay out clothes and a thermos of coffee the night before and fix a blender breakfast in the morning. Not here, where I unbuild the house first.

At least the packing was now a well-rehearsed ballet: The tide is incoming, so estimate the distance it will rise up the beach. Carry the small items and the four large bags down to the staging area, about 20 feet from the water. Try to lay them on seaweed or on bare rock so they won't adhere to sandy gravel and drop it in the boat. Untie the boat from its forest mooring, carry it down, and lay it with just the bow in the water. Loop the lifeline over a rock. Stuff the wine bottle – if one has lasted this long – into its cool cellar in the bow. Put the water bag on top of it, then the foot pump. The boat needed as much weight as possible in the bow and stern to offset the sag of my weight in the center.

All this I do straddling the boat and facing shore, with the water calf-deep on my boots. That way I can pull all the gear firmly toward me under the bow spray cover. Then I lay in the heavy blue waterproof bag, which contains the library, tools, clothing, and kitchen. Tuck the day's water bottle just behind the inflated seat cushion. Snaphook the clear plastic chart holder to a side loop and lay it on top of the blue bag. By now, the water is amidships.

Straddling the stern, I load in the tapered plastic kayak bag, which holds lunches and dinners, carefully tucking it back over the boat's air valves so as not to get a sudden whoosh of deflation. Pick up the fourth bag, which contains tent, tarp, air mattress, and sleeping bag. Snaphook one end of a line to its bottom grommet and the other end to a spray-cover lacing. That fourth bag is my treasured black rubber Navy bag, which also serves as a backrest.

Put on the yellow, bibbed foul-weather pants. Lay the yellow jacket on top of the black bag if it's not raining. If it is, I'll already be wearing both, put on just before I derigged the overhead tarp. Loop the strap of the camera over my head and under my right arm. Now the boat is afloat. Lay the paddle crosswise on top of the chart bag. Check to see that the paddle line is hooked to the boat, as I left it last night. The paddle will float, but with no spare, I can't afford to lose it. Unhook the lifeline from the rock and loop it over my head and under my left arm. Move the boat out to an eight-inch depth. Get in and paddle out, watching carefully for submerged rocks.

Someday I'll manage to do it all just that neatly, instead of having an outgoing tide leave the boat stranded aground just as I've got it all packed, so that I have to unpack and start again. You don't drag these fragile craft.

I moved out past the boats that were fishing in an oval pattern along the coast. My chart was a large-scale one that stopped out in midchannel, but somewhere across Icy Strait, in the pale outline of land that I could see, was the town of Hoonah.

I paddled past a "cabin" on the topo map. No sign of it. On to a reef point covered with the silver gray of gulls. They eyed me warily, then lifted off like a feathered flying carpet, leaving only the barren rocks. I cleared Ainsley Island to my right, then paddled on into a tide race at the north tip of an islet. Powering through and landing, I searched for a camp, but all sites were miserably wet and rocky. The only asset was a bed of beach asparagus to pick for dinner, but I wasn't looking for delicacies, only necessities. A camp or cabin was rumored to be in the bight of Couverden Island, so I paddled down against the wind and rain, but found only bog. Under the alders I sat on a wet rock, visor dripping, and lunched on crackers, tuna, and Tang.

One hundred and two years earlier, John Muir, Hall Young, and a group of Indians had paddled through this area, also en route from Glacier Bay up Lynn Canal. Even when wet and cold during his travels, Muir was using such phrases as "the wind made wild melody," "the shining weather in the midst of rain," and "the glad rejoicing storm in glorious voice was singing through the woods, noble compensation for mere body discomfort." As I hunkered down, glum, soggy, and disconsolate, I thought of Muir's writing, then suddenly exploded with laughter, spewing wet cracker crumbs onto the yellow pants. Muir had made his voyages between 1879 and 1899, but it was not until 1914 that he wrote his journals into the book *Travels in Alaska*. The previous spring I had obsessed over the beauty of this country. Already forgotten was the memory of what bloody hard work a short expedition had been only the summer before. Possibly even the great Muir, who had often gone into the wilderness with only a blanket and a crust of bread, had forgotten some of the misery as he wrote his book 15 years later in front of a fireplace in California.

Heartened, I paddled out of the bight. A powerboat, the *Tiller Tramp*, chartered for fishing out of Juneau, came in from what they described as a "rough channel" and anchored. I paddled out from the quiet shelter of the tip of Couverden into Lynn Canal, the water under my elbow changing in 10 strokes from calm blue bay to a steep, sloppy green sea with a south wind of 25 knots. I looked south, upwind, judged the seas, figured the boat could handle them, and headed north, seas breaking around the boat as it slid down the face of the waves. This boat had no rudder, but with its rocker bottom, like a white-water kayak's, it was responsive instantly to a pull, a brace, or a backwater stroke. We slewed and skidded and raced along, just far enough to see the long coastline to the north, then came ashore.

I shoved through the thick alder and tangled shore brush into a young spruce forest. The only spot that was flat and clear enough to pitch a tent was in the middle of a small path. There were no bear-crap piles or tracks. It looked like a mink or deer trail. It was getting dark at nine o'clock these evenings, especially in a dark forest like this. Still raining.

After rigging three corners for the tarp, I looked for an overhead branch to toss a line over to pull the center loop into a four-sided roof. In the dim light one looked suitable. I tied a rock to the end of a line, threw it up and over the branch, knotted the other end to the tarp loop and hauled. The branch bent down and released a huge dead treetop that had fallen and snagged on the branch. It hurtled past my shoulder and crashed on the side of the tarp, puncturing it with a jagged limb and snapping one corner line. Loggers call them widow makers, justifiably.

I cleared the debris, taped the tarp, rerigged the lines, and made a fast dinner by candlelight.

September 2. I was fixing breakfast and heard a squirrel chatter. Like a small kid trying to pull a big beach umbrella, she was dragging a giant mushroom by the stem, until it broke off. Undaunted, she grabbed one edge in her teeth, ran forward, looking to me like a small Ubangi bulldozer with the mushroom as her lip disk, and disappeared with her prize. (Later I read an article that said it wasn't the Ubangi, but the African Sara and also South American Suya, who wore lip disks; I often think that half our information is misinformation.)

Half an hour later I had the tarp down and was derigging the tent, standing sideways on the trail. A dark shape came up over the rise to the north. I gasped in surprise, gave an *ohh* of appreciation, and froze. The black wolf came loping home from the morning hunt, tongue swinging, alert, assured. I straightened, skin prickling in a primitive reaction. His glance took me in with instant comprehension of all that I represented. His fluid pace did not slacken nor his paws miss a step, but he veered off the trail, through the forest, and was gone. The camera was hanging on a tree. I stepped toward it, then dropped my hand.

Like the encounter with the orca, this was a treasure to hold in my mind, forever to recall with gratitude. I had always thought of wolves as gray and the size of a German shepherd. This one was black and the size of a Great Dane. I had read David Mech and Lois Crisler, and later I would read *Of Wolves and Men*, by Barry Lopez. "Many people in Alaska," he wrote, "hunters, biologists, native people – volunteered the information that the biggest wolves they'd seen were blacks." And: "Here is an animal capable of killing a man, an animal of legendary endurance and spirit, an animal that embodies marvelous integration with its environment. This is exactly what the frustrated modern hunter would like: the noble qualities imagined; a sense of fitting into the world. The hunter wants to be the wolf."

I wasn't and I didn't, but I felt akin to the wolf. It seemed somehow as if we recognized each other in that brief meeting, acknowledged each other without fear as solo animals of different breeds, and went our separate ways. We weren't communicating in human words, but in the tone of voice, gesture, stance, scent, and movement. Was all this a part of some system of interspecies awareness? As much as anything else on this voyage, I wanted that sense of fitting in, coexisting with the animal world.

Two years later I read in a newspaper item that in Alaska the mass killing of wolves from airplanes and helicopters had been approved "in order to save an adequate number of moose." An adequate number for the hunters. I knew it was supposed to be part of a carefully researched plan to maintain populations of animals, but the methods were hard to accept. Maintain which populations for whom?

Mussels Neapolitan

1 cup of dry pasta
3 large or 15 small mussels
¼ cup olive oil
3 cloves garlic, minced

¼ teaspoon hot pepper flakes
4 to 6 dried sliced tomatoes
½ cup dry white wine
2 cans rolled anchovies with capers
parsley or wild greens

Cook pasta and drain. Steam mussels and remove from shells. Save water. Heat oil. Add garlic, cook briefly. Add pepper flakes, tomatoes, wine, and ½ cup mussel water. Cover and cook 10 minutes. Add anchovies, capers, and parsley. Add mussels. Heat only to boiling. Serve over pasta.

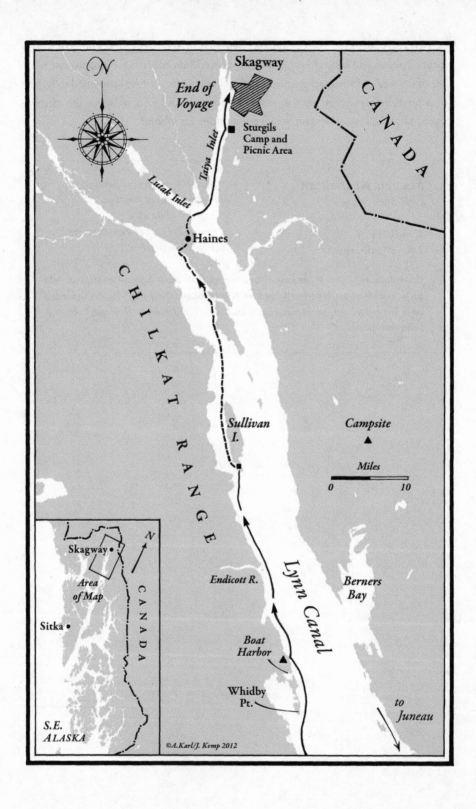

Bears and a Broken Paddle

Looking out from the shelter of the small offshore islands I saw the seas had gone down overnight – down to four feet – but still big enough to demand attention to each wave. I angled over to Point Howard and kept going four more hours. Rain and a tailwind. There was supposed to be a float house in a cove opposite Point Retreat, but when I arrived at low tide, no house, so I tied up and walked into the estuary, then around a curve to a large boggy area. No buildings were in sight, but float house locations are designed to be temporary.

Six miles later I stopped to fill the water bag. It was a good campsite, but there were dozens of salmon swimming upstream, half-eaten ones on the bank, and a pile of bear crap every 20 feet. Go! As I launched from shore, one paddle blade snapped off at the shaft. Was it already cracked from the strain of 80 days under way? Had I hit a rock underwater without knowing it? The broken blade was floating, and I grabbed it. Using one paddle and the old canoeing J stroke, I moved along the shore to a curving beach a quarter mile from the stream. At the end of the beach was a rock cliff. Around it I would be out of the bay, but out into rough water again. With one paddle? Not advisable.

I set up camp, confident that I'd be able to repair the broken paddle, but I needed daylight for the precise careful work if I were not to botch the whole job irredeemably. I couldn't rely on anyone else. I had seen no boats all day, up and down the 40 visible miles of Lynn Canal.

All three pairs of socks were wet, so I wrapped my feet in a pair of wool underwear and wore the spare longies to bed. I was also wearing the wool cap that my sister, Marge, had knitted. A professor of home economics, she was mostly concerned with the administration of a department and with the training of graduate students. Unlike some academic types, she also practiced the skills of carpentry, architectural design, good cooking, and knitting wool caps. On the whole trip, that cap had been the single most useful item. It was my thermostat. Body too warm? Take off my cap. Feet cold? Put on the cap. Fifty percent of a body's heat can be lost through a bare head. I wore it every night, and could therefore use a lighter-weight sleeping bag.

The tarp was overhead, the tent was zipped up, the wool pants and the pile suit were under and over the air mattress for insulation. That Stebco three-quarter-length mattress deserved a citation. It had been left at my house 10 years before by an unknown guest, and since then it had been my bed on coral, on lava, on twigs, and it still endured. It made all the difference between a good night's sleep and mere survival. When it finally wore out, five years later, I could find no comparable lightweight product. Soon after, Cascade Designs had invented the Therm-a-Rest mattress, not the soft comfort of an air mattress, but better insulation.

Propped on my elbows, I looked through the tent screen. Across the channel, Herbert Glacier flowed ponderously down the slope, and the sky was almost clear. On my side of Lynn Canal, Mt. Gulab rose starkly bare above the curve of the beach. I stood looking at it for a long time as it grew dark, watching also for any movement of bears back at the stream across the bay. No tracks were on the sandy beach here. Nineteen miles today; I needed sleep.

The sun rose at 6:00 am. Sunshine – for the moment. I took my mug of coffee out to the beach to see the mountain better. At my feet was something else. A bear's pawprint, seven inches across. Indented in the sand was a paw path, coming toward the tent, then turning toward the sea and back toward the stream. It did not seem from the tracks that this bear had come closer than 50 feet, and it was reassuring to think that they had a set distance. Perhaps she had been curious, had not smelled food as mine was dried and sealed air- and watertight, and had decided that I was female without cubs and therefore not a threat. So she had not needed to be fearful or aggressive, and had gone back about the bear business of catching fish upstream in the shallows. So far, the coexistence theory was working.

Oatmeal for fortitude, and time now to tackle the paddle. I unscrewed the broken stub, pulled it off the aluminum shaft, and put it away. It was surplus now, but that stub of plastic might have a use. I examined the broken blade, and dug out the foam that had kept it floating yesterday. At the base of the foam core was an inner ridge of hard plastic that stopped the end of the shaft at its original depth. OK, I'd have to either make the shaft smaller or the blade hole larger to reconnect the two. I could try heating the end of the metal shaft on the stove and ramming it into the hole to melt the plastic ridge. I refueled the stove, put on a glove as a pot holder, and carefully heated the shaft, then quickly rammed it into the blade, turning as I shoved it down. I could melt and ream out an eighth of an inch at a time, then pull the shaft out, scrape the melted edge with the knife blade, and reheat the shaft. I got about two inches done of the four inches needed. On the last insertion, I didn't keep turning it fast enough, and it stuck. I tried heating the shaft and pulling. I tried holding the shaft and pushing with both feet on the shoulders of the blade. It was firmly stuck. Fine. If it's really going to stay there, I've achieved the objective.

I took the paddle down to the water's edge and stroked it hard back and forth in the cold sea. Would the coldness contract the sections so that it would come apart? It did not. A month later, at home in Hawai'i, I lifted the paddle off its wall hooks, and the blade fell off. Sometimes you are certain that your gear has a brain and soul of its own.

All the time I was working, a corner of my mind was still wrestling with bears. This was to be the last pawprint, the closest I would come to actually seeing a grizzly on this voyage. All of the concern and worry, all of the snapping twigs, all of the evidence, and yet not even a distant sighting of one.

156

A death or two and several maulings do occur each year in Alaska, but it was not until two years later that I had a close meeting. I was to camp at an old cabin in Holkham Bay, 50 miles south of Juneau, en route to the fjord known as Fords Terror. I took my pot of pasta outside and sat there, reading and watching the turquoise icebergs float across the seas. My journal records the episode:

There was no sound, no twig snapped, but I turned and looked over my shoulder. A grizzly bear was standing on the path, 18 feet away, looking at me with golden eyes. It wasn't a big bear, perhaps only 400 or 500 pounds. I stood up slowly. Don't run from a bear – they run 30 miles an hour. Why scream – no one will hear you. Don't startle this bear. Try a quiet conversation.

The usual rapid-fire words were slow and precise.

"How come you're so close? The literature says bears stop at 75 feet, turn sideways and pose to show you how big they are. You're messing up the literature, and do you mind if I come two steps closer to get my camera hanging by the door? I'll need a photo of what ate me."

She looked at me calmly, then turned around, moving stiffly and precisely as if she, too, was uncertain in this situation. At the click of the camera she glanced back, I snapped a second photo then she padded slowly away on the trail through the bushes. She didn't seem aggressive, just visiting and checking to see who was in her territory.

Three days later I would return from Fords Terror, unpack, and walk that trail to the stream. I had thoroughly established my scent on that path four days ago. Now, walking the trail, I sang loudly.

"The bear went over the mountain, the bear ... "

I stopped. There was a large bear pile on the path, precisely erasing my spot, thoroughly reestablishing her territory.

Two-thirty in the afternoon I was having lunch, inside the cabin this time. The doorknob rattled and turned, five feet from my table. I could see her head through the thin plastic sheet on the door, holding the knob in her teeth and turning it. I snatched the camera and took photos, talking all the while.

"Really, this is too much. No, I'm not going to open the door and invite you in. Tomorrow I'll be leaving and the territory will be all yours again. Now go away."

She turned and ambled off down the beach.

I had expected her head to butt clean through the plastic sheet, and later included a huge bear-face photo like that in slide shows.

But now, on this first voyage, with only the rueful awareness that the bears knew me pretty well and I didn't know them at all, I packed and launched with the incoming tide, out around the rock cliffs named the Lynn Sisters. Farther south, down in

Frederick Sound, are the Brothers. As always, I wondered what the Indian names for all these places were, and that led me to wondering what the name for the inhabitants of the Americas would have been if Columbus had not believed that he had reached an outlying island of India.

Did John Cabot, looking for a route to Mecca, call them Indians? Cabot himself was an Italian, Giovanni Caboto of Genoa, who moved to London and was commissioned by Henry VII to explore "the islands west of Ireland." What did the Vikings call them? Did St. Brendan of Ireland have a name for the people he found in the New World? There should be some better name for the native peoples of the Americas. DEAP, Descendants of Early Aboriginal Peoples, seems unlikely to come into popular usage. Inuit means simply "the People." "Americans" has been assumed by the residents of the United States of America, but there are also the United States of Brazil and the United States of Mexico. It seems doubtful that we shall ever achieve the United States of the World.

Musing, I kept paddling, and the sun kept shining. Around Whidby Point I stopped and spread out the sleeping bag, tent, and tarp to dry. The wool socks were laid out too, but they would take longer. Impregnated with saltwater, they'd need to first be thoroughly rinsed with freshwater. By the time I got to a stream again, there would probably be no sunshine.

The tide had turned and was now moving strongly against me. It took three hours to paddle the four miles to Boat Harbor. There was supposed to be a beach a mile beyond it. The harbor itself looked good on the topo, but the entrance was narrow, half the width of the slot into the bay of Hole in the Wall, near Point Baker, and the tide was racing out like rapids in a river.

At 8:30 pm the sun had set, and it was getting dark. Now, in September, there were no more long twilights. I made a small bet that within 20 minutes of landing at the beach ahead, I would have the gear and the boat carried up to a flat area and would be sipping hot soup. I won the bet, had the kitchen laid out on a long chunk of 12 by 12 timber, had a small log to sit on and a branch wedged upright to hold the water bag. Those wine-box bags were wonderfully adaptable; the bag that held my water had an ingenious one-hand spigot; the one I used for a seat was filled with air instead of water, and its aluminized surface reflected my body heat. If I'd had a crab trap, I'd have used a spare bag as a buoy for the line. Two of them laced together could make a float to stick one end of my paddle into; the other end, atop the boat, forming an outrigger to steady the boat for reentry in case of capsize. A float with a hook might hold your bathing suit while you skinny-dipped – a dissertation could be written on the use of wine-box bags.

The tent and tarp went up while dinner cooked. When the full moon rose over the mountain ridge across Lynn Canal, I took a timed photo. It had been an eventful two days. Widow maker, bulldozer squirrel, wolf, bears, a broken and mended paddle, sunshine, and now a moonrise for the first time in a month of clouded skies.

Being alone was still satisfying. After so many years of jobs and children, not coping every day with dozens of problems was a luxury. Space to think. May Sarton has said, "With another human being present, vision becomes double vision, inevitably. We are busy wondering, what does my companion see or think of this, and what do I think of it? The original impact gets lost or diffused." The concept of meditation recognized the need; if you couldn't be physically isolated, you could try for a mental space. Americans are said to have a love affair with automobiles, but it may be only their need for solitude, if one of those enclosed boxes is the only place they can achieve it. There has to be some time when the brain can synapse the ideas already there into lateral and diagonal connections without constant new bombardment.

"But are you safe alone?" people ask. I'm certain that I am safer.

Safety is more good judgment than reliance on people. Each day as I packed I kept going through the what-ifs, and preparing for them. "When in doubt, don't" was a good rule. Alone, I could meticulously prepare for launching, checking how and where to stow each item, keeping the emergency gear at hand. No one rushed or distracted me. Nothing except tide or wind timed the departure or told me what to do. I didn't have to risk my life rescuing someone else. On earlier group expeditions I had loaned critical gear because people neglected to bring their own. They snapped my knife blade, left my books and charts in the rain, burned the nozzle off my foot pump using it as a fire bellows, and sliced my boat dragging it out of their way. Animals were less dangerous than humans.

"But aren't you afraid alone?" Of what? Fear is of the unknown. I had almost learned what the boat, the gear, and the body could do. Even the sea and the weather followed patterns. I was still learning, but all the percentage figures said I was safer here than in a city or on a highway.

In a few days the voyage would be over. What would be next? Before I left home I had rewritten the lists: income and outgo for the next five years, 25 things I really wanted to do, how much they would cost, and their priorities on a one to five scale. What was the five-year plan, the 25-year plan? How much time could I reasonably expect to have before physical deterioration set in? When I was five years old, the time-was-there-was-time palindrome of endless years stretched ahead. One year was a big 20 percent of my whole life, so a year was a very long time. By the time I was 30, the ratio had shrunk. One thirtieth of my life was a very short time, and it whizzed past.

What were the main issues I believed in, the big problems the world faced? By now I didn't believe the world was getting better, only more complicated and less likely to survive. Still, we all need to go down fighting, lost cause or not, backs against the wall. The biggest issue seemed to me to be overpopulation. OK, go home and enlist in the battles. I was an unlikely Cyrano or Don Quixote, and there were many truly valiant and capable people doing battle.

Age was also relative. At 29 you say 30 isn't old, but 40 is. At 59 you say 60 isn't old, but 70 is. At 89, a lovely friend is saving for her old age. Some mornings after I've

been in the ocean in Hawai'i, I feel 14, and when I glance in a mirror I stop, stunned. "Who is that?"

Part sun, part cloud, a little rain, and the vast empty channel with its high snow-capped ridge of peaks on the far side. On my side I was too close in to see beyond the first slope up to the high spine of mountains that I knew was there from the maps. Ahead was Danger Point, and as I paddled close I could understand the name. A ledge jutted far out into the channel, just under the water for much of the tidal range, just deep enough to be unseen, and shallow enough to tear the bottom out of a boat. It was good mussel habitat, though, the crust of shells so thick I couldn't see the rock. I nudged up to the opalescent, deep-blue wall that towered over my head on this low tide, estimated that it would be three feet under at high tide, and backed away from the sharp lips of the shells.

Ahead was the Endicott River and a tidal flat, a fan-shaped delta of gravel and rocks brought down by the flows of centuries. I had planned to stop at four o'clock, when the tide would turn against me, but by three a southeast wind was blowing enough to offset the tide. It was 10 more miles to Sullivan Island and a reported house. In another hour I'd be able to see the shape, far ahead. The tailwind was 15 knots, the seas only three feet, and the rain was light, so I kept moving. I was using painkill-ers every day now, knowing that I might be doing permanent damage to muscles and tendons, knowing also the recuperative power of this body, trading off the possibility of damage against the desire to reach the goal of Skagway.

I passed Sullivan River, but the freshwater was far upstream. The house ahead looked big and elegant. Would it be a summer home for residents of Haines or Juneau, all furnished and bolted against stray paddlers? Only as I made a backwater stroke and glided to a halt at the shore could I see that the windows were gone and that it was only the shell of a very old building.

I carried up the first load, set it down outside, and walked quietly into the presence of all the adults and children who had once lived there. Peeling wallpaper in the bath-room revealed newspapers and comic strips of the 1920s. It was like the house where I lived when I was five, near the railroad station in Zelzah, now Northridge, in southern California. This one, too, had a fireplace, a pantry, and a wide stairway up to bed-rooms on the top floor. I set up my kitchen here on a similar second-story sun porch, then walked again through the house with a pot of pasta primavera in hand, listening to the remembrance of things past. At the foot of the stairs I paused, seeing in my mind a pool of blood. Weak from kidney disease, my father had crashed backward, hitting his head on the bottom step in that childhood house. After his death we moved away, but the plan of the house, the fig tree with sheltering branches to the ground making a leaf-walled playhouse for a small girl, Papa milking the cow in the barn, the pines of the mountains where we spent the summers – the images were forever implanted.

I rigged the tarp outside in a ground hollow to catch rainwater, put the sleeping bag and mattress in the back pantry, where there was the least wind blowing through, and wrote the journal for the day. My hand was tingling and numb; a paddling callus inside the thumb gripped the pen. The dirt under the fingernails was Alaska dirt, and I was already homesick for each campsite of the voyage.

Twenty miles north and a day later in the town of Haines, the radio forecast was for a 25-knot northerly wind. It sounded like the onset of winter, the beginning of the noted storms of Skagway, coming down from the Arctic through the Yukon territory and funneling down the valley through Skagway into Lynn Canal. Today I had planned to paddle the final 17 miles. Could I get to Skagway ahead of the storm? There were no landings, no beaches along this last gorge. Weather forecasts were usually accurate as to content. Only the time of arrival of the wind and rain varied from the reports. If I couldn't make it into a northerly wind, at least I could turn and come back downwind.

I headed out and across Lutak Inlet, then around the point. No outlets were ahead, no straits, no exits, only land up there at the end of Taiya Inlet, the northeast final arm of Lynn Canal. There was a 10-knot northerly headwind and an outgoing tide the first hour, then a gradual tide change. I crossed the mile over to the east side in the steady rain. There were no landings for going ashore, just steep rock walls. Only once did I find a rock low enough so that I could climb out for a pit stop. Steady paddling. Lunch of a granola bar, a mint patty, and an orange I found floating. The boat had two quarts of water in it from the rain, but there was no place now to stop and unload to turn it over and empty it. I sopped up what I could with the sponge and squeezed it overboard.

The ferry *Columbia* passed me, heading south. I was fearful of the wake, but she was out in midchannel, her waves only two feet high, and not steep or breaking at this distance of half a mile. I had run off my last chart, but figured where I was on the topo map from the shape of the waterfalls and the angles of their steep courses down the cliffs.

I kept watching ahead through the rain, counting ridges. There were at least three to pass, plus a doubtful one that might be the last toe between Skagway and the old town of Dyea where the Chilkoot Trail of the 1898 gold rush began. Knowing the total distance, I figured I should be in Skagway by 6:00 pm. Finally a small boat ahead turned right and disappeared in front of the last ridge. I knew now. There was only an hour left of the voyage.

To my right were a cleft, a stream, and the familiar brown and yellow carved wooden sign of the Forest Service. I came ashore on the rocks. Sturgils Camp and Picnic Area, the lettering said. A trail wound inland, and heavy wooden tables were set up on a small flat with a view down the inlet. I went back to the boat and pulled out from the bow the wine that I bought the previous night in Haines. I climbed back up to the tables, uncorked the bottle, held it out in salute to Lynn Canal, then drank a toast to that one view and to all the memorable views I had seen. I toasted the whole voyage, the rain, Alaska, the dark forests, all the animals I had met and all the ones I hadn't, the sea, and finally:

"To Aud. You did OK."

The rain eased into a mist. The mountains were clear. Each needle, each scent, each pebble was sharp and singular. Across the inlet a glacier spilled over a high ridge, its crevasses an electric blue. I recorked the bottle, mist and tears and wine dripping off my chin, then went back to the boat and paddled on. The wind had shifted. On this last mile I would have a tailwind, a final gift from the sea.

I rounded the last point. A warehouse was ahead, then the huge bulky stern of a cruise ship. Only a few passengers were on deck in their raincoats, slouch hats, and plastic bonnets. They scarcely glanced down at my boat and its soggy 60-year-old paddler. Adventure was only relative. The ship was theirs, this boat was mine, and I would not trade. I slowed the stroke, savoring, and paddled on into the small boat harbor. Then, barely moving, I stroked around the cemented dock, past the moored skiffs, and glided to a stop at the foot of the shore ramp.

I put the paddle up on the dock, then a knee, and rolled out. I unclipped the lifeline, used it to tie the boat to a cleat, and looked around, north toward the Arctic, up at the mountains. The first snow of winter was on the slopes, the alders were turning gold, the last flowers of the fireweed were at the top of the stalk, and the journey was over. I pulled out the half bottle, uncorked it and looked down at the yellow boat. Eighty-five days, 850 miles.

I poured the last of the wine over the bow.

"Well done, small boat."

BIBLIOGRAPHY:
Books Mentioned in the Text

Bateson, Gregory, *Steps to an Ecology of Mind*, University of Chicago Press, 2000

Beard, Daniel Carter, and Lloyd Khan, *Shelters, Shacks, and Shanties*, FQ Books, 2010

Bohn, Dave, *Glacier Bay: The Land and the Silence*, Alaska Geographic Association, 1992

Caldwell, Francis E., and Robert DeArmond, *Land of the Ocean Mists: The Wild Ocean Coast West of Glacier Bay,* Anchor Publishing Co., 1996

Conrad, Joseph, *Typhoon*, CreateSpace, 2011

Cooper, David J., *Brooks Range Passage*, The Mountaineers Books, 1982

Dana, Richard Henry, *Two Years Before the Mast*, Penguin Group (USA) Inc., 2009

Dowd, John, *Sea Kayaking: A Manual for Long-Distance Touring*, D&M Publishers, Inc., 2004

Edey, Maitland, *The Northeast Coast*, Time-Life, Inc., 1972

Fradkin, Philip L., *Wildest Alaska: Journeys of Great Peril in Lituya Bay*, UC Press, 2003

Gibbons, Euell, *Beachcomber's Handbook*, David McKay Co., 1967 (Field Guide edition)

Gibbons, Euell, *Stalking the Blue-Eyed Scallop*, Alan C. Hood & Co. Inc., 1988

Graves, John, *Goodbye to a River: A Narrative*, Knopf Doubleday Publishing Group, 2002

The Guinness Book of Records, Peter Matthas, ed., Bantam Books, New York, 1996

Hadman, Ballard, *As the Sailor Loves the Sea*, Trafford Publishing, 1999

Hilson, Stephen E., *Evergreen Pacific: Exploring Alaska and British Columbia*, Evergreen Pacific Publishing, Ltd., 1997

Lewis, David, *Ice Bird: The Classic Story of the First Single-Handed Voyage to Antarctica*, Sheridan House, Inc., 2002

Lewis, David, *We, The Navigators: The Ancient Art of Landfinding in the Pacific*, University of Hawai'i Press, 1994

Lopez, Barry, *Of Wolves and Men*, Scribner, 2004

Manning, Harvey, *The Wild Cascades*, Sierra Club, 1965

Maxwell, Gavin, *Ring of Bright Water*, R. Godine Publisher, 2011

McPhee, John, *Coming into the Country*, Farrar Straus & Giroux, 1991

McPhee, John, *Giving Good Weight*, Farrar, Straus & Giroux, 1994

Morton, Alexandra, *Listening to Whales: What the Orcas Have Taught Us*, A Ballantine Book, 2002

Mudd-Ruth, Maria, *Rare Bird: Pursuing the Mystery of the Marbled Murrelet*, Rodale Press, Inc., 2005

Muir, John, *Travels in Alaska*, BiblioBazaar, 2009

Neale, Tom, *An Island to Oneself*, Ox Bow Press, 1990

Payne, Roger, *Among Whales*, Charles Scribner's Sons, 1995

Piggott, Margaret, *Discover Southeast Alaska with Pack and Paddle*, The Mountaineers Books, 1990

Raban, Jonathan, *Passage to Juneau: A Sea and its Meanings*, Knopf Doubleday Publishing Group, 2000

Rearden, Jim, *Alaska Mammals*, Alaska Geographic Series, Graphic Arts Center Publishing Co., 1981

Roppel, Patricia, *Southeast, Alaska's Panhandle*, Alaska Geographic Society, 1978

Searby, Ellen, and Henry Jori, *Alaska's Inside Passage Traveler: See More, Spend Less*, Windham Bay Press, 1999

Service, Robert W., *Collected Poems*, Putnam Adult, 1989

Severin, Tim, *The Brendan Voyage*, Gill & MqcMillan Ltd., 2005

Stevenson, Robert Louis, *An Inland Voyage*, John Beaufoy Publishing, 2011

Stevenson, Robert Louis, *Travels with A Donkey in the Cevennes*, Tutis Digital Publishing Private Ltd., 2008

Sutherland, Audrey, *Paddling My Own Canoe*, University of Hawai'i Press, 1978

Vancouver, George, *Voyage of Discovery to the North Pacific Ocean and Round the World*, Da Capo Press, 1967

Walker, T. J., *Red Salmon, Brown Bear; the Story of an Alaska Lake, Based on the Experiences of Dr. Theodore J. Walker*, World Pub., 1971

Waring, Gerald A., *Thermal Springs of the United States and Other Countries of the World*, U.S. Geological Survey Professional Paper, 4 92 Washington D.C., 1965

White, E. B., *Essays of E. B. White*, Harper & Row, 1977

White, E. B., *Stuart Little*, HarperCollins, 2000

Wik, Ole, *Woodstoves: How to Make Them and Use Them*, Alaska Northwest Books, 1977

Wright, Billie, *Four Seasons North*, Peter Smith Publisher, Inc., 1995

BIBLIOGRAPHY:
Other Useful Books

Armstrong, Robert H. and Marge Hermans, *Alaska's Natural Wonders: A Guide to the Phenomena of the Far North*, Graphic Arts Center Publishing Co., 2000

Barr, Lou and Nancy, *Under Alaskan Seas*, Graphic Arts Center Publishing Co., 1983

Burch, David, *Fundamentals of Kayak Navigation: Master the Traditional Skills and the Latest Technologies*, Globe Pequot Press, 2008

Childs, Craig, *Crossing Paths: Uncommon Encounters with Animals in the Wild*, Sasquatch Books, 1997

Daniel, Linda, *Kayak Cookery: A Handbook of Provisions and Recipes*, Globe Pequot Press, 1998

Fortner, Heather J., *The Limu Eater: A Cookbook of Hawaiian Seaweed*, University of Hawai'i Sea Grant College Program, 1978

Frazer, Neil, *Boat Camping Haida Gwaii: A Small Vessel Guide*, Harbour Publishing Co, Inc., 2010

Heacox, Kim, *Alaska's Inside Passage*, Graphic Arts Center Publishing, 2001

Hoshino, Michio, *Grizzly*, Chronicle Books LLC, 1987

Kirchhoff, M. J., *Baranof Island*, Alaska Cedar Press, 1990

Klein, Tom et al., *Loon Magic*, T&N Children's Publishing, 1996

Nickerson, Sheila, *Disappearance, a Map: A Meditation on Death and Loss in the High Latitudes*, Houghton Mifflin Harcourt Trade & Reference Publishers, 1997

O'Clair, Rita, Robert H. Armstrong, and Richard Carstensen, *The Nature of Southeast Alaska: A Guide to Plants, Animals and Habitats*, Graphic Arts Center Publishing Co., 1998

Orth, Donald J., and Marcus Baker, *Dictionary of Alaska Place Names*, U.S. Geological Survey Professional Paper 567, Washington, D.C., 1967

Stall, Chris et al., *Pacific Northwest*, The Mountaineers Books, 1981

Schofield, Janice, *Alaska's Wild Plants: A Guide to Alaska's Edible Harvest*, Graphic Arts Center Publishing Co., 1993

Schooler, Lynn et al., *The Blue Bear: A True Story of Friendship and Discovery in the Alaskan Wild*, HarperCollins Publishers, 2003

Short, Wayne, *The Cheechakoes*, Devil's Thumb Press, 1995

Smith, Dave, *Backcountry Bear Basics: The Definitive Guide to Avoiding Unpleasant Encounters*, The Mountaineers Books, 1997

Taylor, Raymond F., *Pocket Guide to Alaska's Trees*, U.S. Dept. of Agriculture, Forest Service, 1950

Wild, Edible, and Poisonous Plants of Alaska, Cooperative Extension Services, University of Alaska, 1993

Upton, Joe, *Journeys Through the Inside Passage: Seafaring Adventures along the Coast of British Columbia and Alaska*, Graphic Arts Center Publishing Co., 2008

Gear List

Shelter and Sleeping
Tent & ground cloth
Tarp & nylon cord
Sleeping bag & cover
Air mattress & Therm-a-Rest

Photography
Camera, tripod, & film
Batteries

Transportation
Plane ticket
Airline bags **
Boat & paddle
Pump & pack towel
Spray decks
Lifeline & paddle tether
Charts, maps, chart bags, compass
Seat cushion, life jacket
Repair & tool kit
Waterproof bags
Ferry schedule
Tide book

Food and Kitchen
Kitchen bag (stove & utensils)
Water bag
Fuel canisters
Thermos
Food in bags
Water/juice bottle

Emergency Gear
VHF & weather radio & batteries
Flares
Lighters
Plastic sheet (drop cloth)
Fire starters
Space blanket
Signal light
Waterproof flashlight

Clothing and Personal Gear
Nylon fast-drying pants *
Polo shirt * (fast dry)
Tennies *
Pile Jacket *
Pile pants
Foul-weather jacket & pants
3 sets nylon underwear (wear one)
3 pairs socks (wear one)
Knee-high Xtra Tuff boots
Inner soles
Knit watch cap & gloves
Fleece pullover
Towel
First-Aid medical kit
Personal kit

Miscellany
Pocket desk (wallet)
Credit card & money
Driver's license
Address book & stampsHook & knife sharpener
Pen & pencil
Thermometer
Journal & notepad
Binoculars
Reading & dark glasses
Knife
Books, reading & reference
Flashlight & batteries
Saw, hatchet, pry bar, nails
Trash bags
Sewing kit
Waterproof watch
Spare lighters

* Wear from home
** After arrival, mail to town of departure

ACKNOWLEDGEMENTS

During the years from 1980 to 2003 I paddled each summer in Southeast Alaska. These people were helpful at different times and in many ways.

John Booth, Mary and Jerry Castle, John Dowd, John Dutton, Heather Fortner, Neil Frazer, Ken Leghorn, Sanford Lung, Michelle Masden, Pauline McNeil, and Mark Rognstad.